ADULT EDUCATION

A Practical Guide for Educators, Trainers and Researchers

ADULT EDUCATION
A Practical Guide for Educators, Trainers and Researchers

Dr A B Sinha

MD PUBLICATIONS PVT LTD
NEW DELHI
www.mdppl.com

Published by :

MD Publications Pvt Ltd
"MD House", 11, Darya Ganj,
New Delhi - 110 002
Phone : +91-11-45355555
E-mail : contact@mdppl.com
Website: www.mdppl.com

ISBN : 978-81-7533-364-2

Published and Printed by Mr. Pranav Gupta on behalf of **MD Publications Pvt Ltd** at Mohit Enterprises, Delhi.

PREFACE

Adult Education had a diversity of meanings attached to it in the selected countries. Primarily it was considered a second chance for education for those who could not get mainstream schooling. Adult education in these countries was for the down trodden, unreachable and disadvantaged group for whom popular primary education was not possible as these groups were socially, culturally and economically marginalized. The content of adult education was varied in the selected countries and consisted of literacy, development messages and employment-oriented skills. The concept of adult education has been evolving, depending upon the literacy status of population, which in general determines the goals, targets, literacy levels and the phase of development the country was going through.

Adult Education is the action of an external educational agent in purposefully ordering behavior into planned systematic experiences that can result in learning for those for whom such an activity is supplemental to their primary role in society and which involves some continuity in an exchange relationship between the agent and the learner so that the educational process is under constant supervision and direction.

The programs provide one-to-one tutoring and small group sessions for adults at the 6th grade level or below. Public libraries, nonprofit organizations and school systems administer these programs across the country. Many adult education centers from community colleges receive grants from Welfare and Unemployment departments to offer training to welfare and unemployment recipients to help these individuals gain life and work skills to facilitate their return to the mainstream. They also provide programs for ex-offenders to reintegrate to society.

Educating adults differs from educating children in several ways. One of the most important differences is that adults have accumulated knowledge, work experience or military service that can add to the learning experience. Another difference is that most adult education is voluntary, therefore, the participants are generally better motivated.

Adults frequently apply their knowledge in a practical fashion to learn effectively. They must have a reasonable expectation that the knowledge recently gained will help them further their goals. One example, common in the 1990s, was the proliferation of computer training courses in which adults, most of whom were office workers, could enroll. These courses would teach basic use of the operating system or specific application software. Because the abstractions governing the user's interactions with a PC were so new, many people who had been working white-collar jobs for ten years or more eventually took such training courses, either at their own whim or at the behest of their managers.

I am very grateful to Mr. Pranav Gupta, Director of MD Publications Pvt. Ltd., New Delhi, for his kind cooperation and support for this book.

Dr A B Sinha

CONTENTS

	Preface	*v*
1.	Adult Education: Teaching and Educating Adults	1
2.	Principles and Modelling of Education and Development	43
3.	Community Control and Local Participation in Education	61
4.	Globalization of Adult Education and Training	79
5.	Institutional Framework for Adult Education	97
6.	Conceptual Understandings of Adult Education	117
7.	Developing the Curriculum for Adult Education	131
8.	Organizing Community for Adult Education	151
9.	Challenge to Serve Minority Groups in Adult Education	177
10.	Planning in a Community based Adult Education	207
11.	Adult Education: Fear-Driven Models	227
	Bibliography	241
	Index	245

1

Adult Education: Teaching and Educating Adults

INTRODUCTION

Adult education is the practice of teaching and educating adults. Adult education takes place in the workplace, through 'extension' or 'continuing education' courses at secondary schools, or at colleges or universities. Other learning places include folk high schools, community colleges, and lifelong learning centers. The practice is also often referred to as 'Training and Development' and is often associate with workforce or professional development. It has also been referred to as *andragogy* (to distinguish it from *pedagogy*). Adult education is different from vocational education, which is mostly workplace-based for skill improvement; and also from non-formal adult education, including learning skills or learning for personal development.

CHARACTERISTICS

Programs provide one to one tutoring and small group sessions for adults at the 6th grade level or below. Public libraries, nonprofit organizations and school systems administer these programs across the country.

Educating adults differs from educating children in several ways. One of the most important differences is that adults have accumulated knowledge, work experience or military service that can add to the learning experience. Another difference is that most adult education is voluntary therefore, the participants are generally better motivated.

Adults frequently apply their knowledge in a practical fashion to learn effectively. They must have a reasonable expectation that the knowledge recently gained will help them further their goals. One example, common in the 1990s, was the proliferation of computer training courses in which adults (not children or adolescents), most of whom were office workers, could enroll. These courses would teach basic use of the operating system or specific application software. Because the abstractions governing the user's interactions with a PC were so new, many people who had been working white-collar jobs for ten years or more eventually took such training courses, either at their own whim (to gain computer skills and thus earn higher pay) or at the behest of their managers.

In the United States, a more general example, and stereotypical, is that of the high-school dropout who returns to school to complete general education requirements. Most upwardly-mobile positions require at the very least a high school diploma or equivalent. A working adult is unlikely to have the freedom to simply quit his or her job and go "back to school" full time. Public school systems and community colleges usually offer evening or weekend classes for this reason. In Europe this is often referred to as "second-chance", and many schools offer tailor-made courses and learning programs for these returning learners.

Those adults who read at the very lowest level get help from volunteer literacy programs. These national organizations provide training, tutor certification, and accreditation for local volunteer programs. States often have state organizations such as Literacy Florida Inc., which provide field services for volunteer literacy programs.

In the U.S.A., the equivalent of the high school diploma earned by an adult through these programs is to pass the General Education Development (GED) test.

Another fast-growing sector of adult education is English for Speakers of Other Languages (ESOL), also referred to as English as a Second Language (ESL) or English Language Learners (ELL). These courses are key in assisting immigrants with not only the acquisition of the English language, but the acclimation process to the culture of the United States.

THE BASICS

One of the primary goals of adult education is functional literacy. Organizations like the U.S. Department of Education and the United Nations Educational, Scientific and Cultural Organization (UNESCO) work tirelessly to measure, understand, and address adult illiteracy in the U.S. and around the world.

"Only though adult education can we address the real problems of society like power sharing, wealth creation, gender and health issues," said Adama Ouane, Director of the UNESCO Institute for Lifelong Learning.

Adult Basic Education: In the U.S., each state is responsible for addressing the basic education of their citizens. Official state websites direct people to classes, programs, and organizations designed to teach adults how to read prose, documents like maps and catalogs, and how to make simple computations.

GED: Adults who complete basic adult education have the opportunity to earn the equivalent of a high school diploma by taking the General Educational Development, or GED, test. GED prep resources abound online and in classrooms around the country, designed to help students prepare for the five-part exam.

Beyond the Basics: Beyond the basics, adult education is synonymous with continuing education. The world of lifelong learning is wide open. Whether you are :

- Going to college for the first time after age 25;
- Returning to college to finish a degree;
- Working toward a graduate degree;
- Learning a technical skill;
- Taking classes at your local community centre for the sheer fun of it;

FORMS OF ADULT EDUCATION

Contemporary adult education can take many different forms. Colleges and universities have instituted evening programs, extension work, courses without credit, correspondence courses, and distance learning programs (with courses transmitted by satellite to numerous locations); community colleges have been especially active in this area. Organizations designed to relieve illiteracy are instrumental in adult education, as are the schools established to teach the English language and American customs to the foreign-born. Adult education is also sponsored by corporations, labour unions, and private institutes. The field now embraces such diverse areas as vocational education, high-school equivalency, parent education, adult basic education (including literacy training), physical and emotional development, practical arts, applied science, and recreation as well as the traditional academic, business, and professional subjects. Each year millions of Americans take such a course or program.

At the local level, public schools have been active in furnishing facilities and assistance to private adult education groups in many communities. Community centres, political and economic action associations, and dramatic, musical, and artistic groups are regarded by many as adult education activities. Great Books groups, in which adults read and discuss a specified list of volumes, grew out of great books seminars at Chicago and Columbia universities and St. John's College. In many places the local public library sponsors such groups.

PURPOSES FOR ADULT EDUCATION

As adults we are always learning new things and processing new information. Education in a more systematic way also occurs. The following reasons are often suggested for people to continue to engage in organized learning:

- *Personal growth and development:* According to psychological theories people seek individual self-actualization and wish to promote individual growth. Someone might join a course or educational program for the content but also for contact with other people in an agreeable setting.
- *Social improvement:* Here the emphasis is gaining new knowledge and skills to improve your personal or career situation. The emphasis is placed on the individual within a larger social context. Thus, someone who left school early might want to get a certificate to show basic competency for employment.
- *Organizational effectiveness:* This happens when an employer or another type of organization (e.g., community group, charity, etc.) sponsors learning activities so that members, employees, volunteers, etc. can reach organizational goals. Sometimes these can be organized through on-site human resource development programs, cr individuals and groups of employees might do educational programs through distance education.
- *Intellectual growth:* Many people value learning for

its own sake.

- *Social transformation:* Organizations supporting policy advocacy and social change may wish to reach members through education which changes people and challenges existing social systems.

PRINCIPLES OF ADULT EDUCATION

Whatever mixture of reasons may motivate someone to pursue education and training, effective programs must be directed at adults in a manner that will be useful to their needs and interests. If they are disappointed, they will stop attending. Effective adult education programs:

- Are based on the needs of the participants and make use of their different experiences,
- Seek the participation of individual adults, groups and communities in decision-making at all levels of the learning process; including determination of needs, curriculum development, program implementation and evaluation,
- Use course activities that are practical and problem centred,
- Engage participants in the learning process through an interactive approach,
- Incorporate learners' goals in the activities,
- Use discussion and group activities to help create a supportive educational environment,
- Demonstrate practical applications of the skills and knowledge gained,
- Use logic and sequence of class activities should reinforce lessons learned,
- Demonstrate how the material and concepts learned fit together as a package,
- Allow for self-appraisal opportunities, use of skills learned, and evaluation/feedback to the instructor.

Examples of Adult Education Programs

- Adult basic education,
- Literacy programs,
- Adult secondary education (including high school credit courses, and vocational training for entry-level employment),
- Life-coping skills,
- Parenting skills,
- Citizenship training for immigrants,
- English as a second language,
- Job-seeking skills,
- Classes for public assistance recipients to prepare them for employment.

ADULT EDUCATION

Background

Post-Independence India inherited a system of education which was characterized by large scale inter and intra-regional imbalances. The system educated a select few, leaving a wide gap between the educated and the illiterate. The country's literacy rate in 1947 was only 14 per cent and female literacy rate was abysmally low at 8 per cent. Only one child out of three had an opportunity for enrolment in primary schools. Educational equality was aggravated by economic inequality, gender disparity and rigid social stratification.

Eradication of illiteracy has been one of the major national concerns of the Government of India since Independence. The need for a literate population and universal education for all children in the age group 6-14 was recognized as a crucial input for nation building and was given due consideration in Constitution as well as in the successive five-year plans. A number of significant programmes have been taken up since Independence to eradicate illiteracy among adults. Some of the important programmes have included:

(i) *Social Education:* The main elements were literacy, extension, general education, leadership training and social consciousness. The programme was implemented in the First Five-Year Plan (1951-56).

(ii) *Gram Shikshan Mohim:* Movement for literacy in the rural areas was started in 1959 in Satara district of Maharashtra, and was later extended to other parts of the state. The programme aimed at imparting basic literacy skills within a period of about four months. The programme, however, suffered from a lack of systematic follow-up which resulted in relapse to illiteracy.

(iii) *Farmers' Functional Literacy Project:* Verdan started in 1967-68 as an inter-ministerial project for farmers' training and functional literacy, the project aimed at popularization of high-yielding varieties of seeds through the process of adult education. The programme was confined to 144 districts of the country where nearly 8,640 classes were organized for about 2.6 lakh adults.

(iv) *Non-formal Education:* In the beginning of the Fifth Plan, a programme of non-formal education for 15-25 age-group was launched. Although the scope, content and objective of the non-formal project was clearly spelt out, its understanding in the field was very limited and the programmes actually organized indistinguishable from the conventional literacy programmes.

(v) *Polyvalent Adult Education Centres Workers':* Social Education Institutes and Polyvalent Adult Education Centres were reviewed by a group in 1977, which recommended adoption of Polyvalent Adult Education Centres in the adult education programmes for workers in urban areas. In pursuance of this decision, Shramik Vidyapeeths were set up in the states.

(vi) *Education Commission (1964-66):* The appointment of Education Commission (1964-66) was a significant event in the history of education in India. Among several measures, it recommended that high priority be accorded to ending illiteracy. It urged that adult education be promoted both through "selective" as well "mass approach" and stressed on the active involvement of teachers and students and the wider use of the media for the literacy programmes. The Education Commission also stated that in the world of science and technology, the main objective should be to relate it to life, needs and aspirations of the people so as to make it an instrument of socio-economic and political change.

(vii) *Functional Literacy for Adult Women (FLAW):* The scheme of Functional Literacy for Adult Women (FLAW) was started in 1975-76 in the experimental ICDS project areas. It was gradually expanded along with the expansion of ICDS. By 1981-82, 300 ICDS projects were approved where these FLAW centres also functioned. However, it was decided to stop the expansion of FLAW scheme in ICDS project areas mainly due to a constraint of resources. The aim of FLAW scheme was to enable illiterate adult women to acquire functional skills along with literacy, to promote better awareness of health, hygiene, child-care practices and to bring about attitudinal changes. The target age group was 15-35 age group.

(viii) *National Adult Education Programme (NAEP):* The first nation-wide attempt at eradication of illiteracy was made through the National Adult Education Programme launched on October 2, 1978. It was a massive programme which aimed at educating 100 million non-literate adults in the age group of 15-35 years within a time-frame of five years. The objectives of the National Adult Education Programme were not merely to impart literacy in the conventional sense, but also to provide learners with functional awareness, which were conceived as three integral components of the skills of reading, writing and arithmetic. Functionality implied the ability to utilize and apply the skills acquired with a view to promote efficiency of the neo-literate. The social awareness component aimed at knowing, understanding and taking action on issues which affect the individual, community and society.

(ix) *Rural Functional Literacy Project (RFLP):* This was the flagship programme of NAEP and was started as a centrally-sponsored scheme in 1978 for rural areas. The erstwhile 144 Farmers' Functional Literacy Projects and 60 Non-formal Education Projects were merged into it. Further, projects were added and the number of projects throughout the country in 1987 were 513, each having upto a maximum number of 300 adult education centres and each centre having 25-30 learners.

(x) *State Adult Education Programme (SAEP):* The states also similarly took up centre-based projects under the state plan funds on the lines of RFLPs.

(xi) *Adult Education through Voluntary Agencies:* To ensure greater participation of voluntary agencies, the Central Scheme of Assistance to Voluntary Agencies was revived in April 1982. Under this scheme, registered societies were sanctioned Centre-based projects for functional literacy and post-literacy, where they were allowed to run projects in a compact area.

REVIEW OF THE NATIONAL ADULT EDUCATION PROGRAMME

Intended to be a mass programme, the National Adult Education Programme (NAEP), however, remained a traditional centre-based programme, which was also honorarium based, hierarchical and government-funded and government controlled. As against the target of 100 million, a total of 44.22 million learners were enrolled in adult education centres in different years upto March 1988. On the basis of sample evaluation studies, it has been estimated that about 45 per cent of the enrolled learners attained literacy. The centre-based programme was reviewed and evaluated by several institutes of social science research and later, the Government of India also appointed a review committee headed by Prof. D.S. Kothari to assess the strengths and weaknesses of the programme. The strengths and weaknesses of the NAEP as revealed through various evaluation studies are summarized below:

STRENGTHS

1. Women's motivation and participation has been high.
2. Coverage of weaker sections of the society (SCs and STs) was higher than the target.
3. The project approach to management adopted for adult education programme is feasible.
4. The quality of teaching-learning materials prepared by the National Resource Centre and the State Resource Centres was found to be positive.
5. The programme worked well where special recruitment procedures were adopted.

WEAKNESSES

1. Quality of training of the functionaries was poor.
2. The learning environment in the adult education centres was poor.
3. Mass media did not provide appreciable support.
4. Voluntary agencies did not receive willing cooperation from State Governments.
5. The existing procedures for their involvement were discouraging.

6. There was no linkage between basic literacy, post-literacy, follow-up and continuing education, resulting in the relapse of large number of neo-literates into illiteracy.
7. Achievement levels of literacy were below the desired level.
8. Training of adult education functionaries at all levels lacked participatory and communicative techniques.
9. Political and administrative support of the state governments and the Panchayati Raj institutions was not forthcoming.

National Literacy Mission (NLM) has been conceptualized and built on an objective assessment of the strengths and weaknesses of the earlier programmes emanating from the evaluation study reports. The creation of a mission for literacy represents a national political commitment on the need to harness social forces and channelise the energies of people towards meeting the ultimate objective of effecting a qualitative change in their own lives. Conceptually, the mission focus on:

1. A new sense of urgency, seriousness and emphasis with fixed goals, clear time-frame and age-specific target groups.
2. Firm belief that adults can be made literate according to certain pre-determined norms within a stipulated time limit (200 hours) and that it not too late to learn.
3. Emphasis on the close nexus between literacy of adult parents and enrolment of school-going children, on the one hand, and literacy and infant mortality; immunization and infant mortality, immunization and child care on the other.
4. A special mission which believes that literacy is not the concern of the one ministry or department or agency but is the concern of the entire nation and all sectors of society.
5. Emphasis on institutionalization of post-literacy and continuing education in a big way.
6. A technology mission also in the sense that besides emphasis on improvement of teaching/learning

environment, it lays stress on improvement in the content and process of teaching-learning on a continuing basis.

7. Envisages creation of an effective mission management system to ensure achievement of the mission objectives within a broad framework of flexibility, delegation, decentralization and accountability.
8. Emphasis not on mere enrolment of learners but on attainment of certain predetermined norms and parameters of literacy, numeracy, functionality and awareness.

LITERACY STATUS

WORLD (in million)

	Total	Male	Female
Adult Literacy Rate** (15+) (%)	82	87	77
Adult Illiterates** (15+) in million	780.66	281.04	499.62
Youth literacy rate (15-24) (%)	87	90	84
Young illiterates (in million)	138.97	52.81	86.16
Out of School population (in million)	76.84	33.25	43.59
Source: Education for All – Global Monitoring Report - 2007			

Literacy Status in Some Asian Countries

South Asian Countries

Country	Total Non-Literate Population 15+age (in million)	Literacy Rate 15+ (%)(2000-2004)		
		Total	Male	Female
Maldives	—	96	96	96
Sri Lanka	—	91	92	89
India	268.42	61	73	48
Bhutan	—	--	--	--
Pakistan	48.81	50	63	36
Nepal	7.66	49	63	35
Bangladesh	52.53	43	52	33
Source: Education for All – Global Monitoring Report - 2007				

Other Asian Countries

Country	Total Non-literate Population 15+ age (in millions)	Literacy Rate 15+ (%) (2000)		
		Total	Male	Female
Thailand	3.35	93	95	91
Philippines	3.50	93	93	93
Vietnam	4.90	90	94	87
Malaysia	1.72	89	92	85
Indonesia	15.10	90	94	87
China	87.01	91	95	87
Myanmar	3.20	90	94	86
Iran	10.50	77	84	70
Laos	1.01	69	77	61
Afghanistan	9.04	28	43	13
Source: Education for All – Global Monitoring Report - 2007				

Literacy Status in Nine most Populous Countries

Country	Total Non-literate Population 15+ age	Literacy Rate 15+ (%)		
		Total	Male	Female
Mexico	6.52	91	92	90
Indonesia	15.10	90	94	87
Brazil	17.36	89	88	89
China	87.01	91	95	87
Nigeria	---	---	---	---
India	268.42	61	73	48
Egypt	14.21	71	83	59
Pakistan	48.81	50	63	36
Bangladesh	52.53	43	52	33
Source: Education for All – Global Monitoring Report – 2007				

INDIA

Literacy Scenario in India (As per 2001 Census): Literacy in India has made remarkable strides since Independence. This has been further confirmed by the results of the Census 2001. The literacy rate has increased

Literacy Rate 1951-2001

Census Year	Persons	Male	Female
1951	18.33	27.16	8.86
1961	28.30	40.40	15.35
1971	34.45	45.96	21.97
1981	43.57	56.38	29.76
1991	52.21	64.13	39.29
2001	64.84	75.26	53.67

from 18.33% in 1951 to 64.84% in 2001. This is despite the fact that during the major part of the last five decades there has been exponential growth of the population at nearly 2% per annum. The state-wise literacy rates are given below:

Literacy Rate 7+ Population (Census 200)

S. No.	India/State/UT		Person	Male	Female
	India	Total	64.84	75.26	53.67
		Rural	58.74	70.70	46.13
		Urban	79.92	86.27	72.86
01	JAMMU & KASHMIR	Total	55.52	66.60	43.00
		Rural	49.78	61.65	36.74
		Urban	71.92	80.00	61.98
02	HIMACHAL PRADESH	Total	76.48	85.35	67.42
		Rural	75.08	84.51	65.68
		Urban	88.95	92.04	85.03
03	PUNJAB	Total	69.65	75.23	63.36
		Rural	64.72	71.05	57.72
		Urban	79.10	83.05	74.49
04	CHANDIGARH	Total	81.94	86.14	76.47
		Rural	75.58	80.98	66.37
		Urban	82.64	86.78	77.40
05	UTTARANCHAL	Total	71.62	83.28	59.63
		Rural	68.07	81.78	54.70
		Urban	81.44	87.05	74.77
06	HARYANA	Total	67.91	78.49	55.73
		Rural	63.19	75.37	49.27
		Urban	79.16	85.83	71.34

S. No.	India/State/UT		Person	Male	Female
07	DELHI	Total	81.67	87.33	74.71
		Rural	78.05	86.60	67.39
		Urban	81.93	87.39	75.22
08	RAJASTHAN	Total	60.41	75.70	43.85
		Rural	55.34	72.16	37.33
		Urban	76.20	86.45	64.67
09	UTTAR PRADESH	Total	56.27	68.82	42.22
		Rural	52.53	66.59	36.90
		Urban	69.75	76.76	61.73
10	BIHAR	Total	47.00	59.68	33.12
		Rural	43.92	57.09	29.61
		Urban	71.93	79.94	62.59
11	SIKKIM	Total	68.81	76.04	60.40
		Rural	66.82	74.45	58.01
		Urban	83.91	87.81	79.16
12	ARUNACHAL PRADESH	Total	54.34	63.83	43.53
		Rural	47.83	57.65	36.94
		Urban	78.26	85.19	69.49
13	NAGALAND	Total	66.59	71.16	61.46
		Rural	62.79	67.58	57.52
		Urban	84.74	87.44	81.42
14	MANIPUR (Excl. 3 Sub-divisions)	Total	70.53	80.33	60.53
		Rural	67.29	77.31	56.95
		Urban	79.28	88.71	70.01
15	MIZORAM	Total	88.80	90.72	86.75
		Rural	81.27	84.93	77.26
		Urban	96.13	96.43	95.80
16	TRIPURA	Total	73.19	81.02	64.91
		Rural	69.72	78.40	60.50
		Urban	89.21	93.21	85.03
17	MEGHALAYA	Total	62.56	65.43	59.61
		Rural	56.29	59.24	53.24
		Urban	86.30	89.05	83.50
18	ASSAM	Total	63.25	71.28	54.61
		Rural	59.73	68.22	50.70
		Urban	85.34	89.74	80.24

S. No.	India/State/UT		Person	Male	Female
19	WEST BENGAL	Total	68.64	77.02	59.61
		Rural	63.42	73.13	53.16
		Urban	81.25	86.13	75.74
20	JHARKHAND	Total	53.56	67.30	38.87
		Rural	45.74	60.94	29.89
		Urban	79.14	87.03	69.96
21	ORISSA	Total	63.08	75.35	50.51
		Rural	59.84	72.93	46.66
		Urban	80.84	87.93	72.87
22	CHHATTISGARH	Total	64.66	77.38	51.85
		Rural	60.48	74.09	46.99
		Urban	80.58	89.39	71.11
23	MADHYA PRADESH	Total	63.74	76.06	50.29
		Rural	57.80	71.70	42.76
		Urban	79.39	87.39	70.47
24	GUJARAT	Total	69.14	79.66	57.80
		Rural	61.29	74.11	47.84
		Urban	81.84	88.34	74.50
25	DAMAN & DIU	Total	78.18	86.76	65.61
		Rural	75.83	84.83	59.33
		Urban	82.31	91.12	73.41
26	DADRA & NAGAR HAVELI	Total	57.63	71.18	40.23
		Rural	49.34	64.50	30.83
		Urban	84.36	90.84	74.54
27	MAHARASHTRA	Total	76.88	85.97	67.03
		Rural	70.36	81.93	58.40
		Urban	85.48	91.03	79.09
28	ANDHRA PRADESH	Total	60.47	70.32	50.43
		Rural	54.50	65.35	43.50
		Urban	76.09	83.19	68.74
29	KARNATAKA	Total	66.64	76.10	56.87
		Rural	59.33	70.45	48.01
		Urban	80.58	86.66	74.12
30	GOA	Total	82.01	88.42	75.37
		Rural	79.67	87.37	71.92
		Urban	84.39	89.46	78.98

S. No.	India/State/UT		Person	Male	Female
31	LAKSHADWEEP	Total	86.66	92.53	80.47
		Rural	85.04	91.49	78.27
		Urban	88.62	93.77	83.13
32	KERALA	Total	90.86	94.24	87.72
		Rural	90.04	93.63	86.69
		Urban	93.19	95.94	90.62
33	TAMIL NADU	Total	73.45	82.42	64.43
		Rural	66.21	77.15	55.28
		Urban	82.53	88.97	75.99
34	PONDICHERRY	Total	81.24	88.62	73.90
		Rural	73.98	83.50	64.38
		Urban	84.84	91.18	78.57
35	ANDAMAN & NICOBAR ISLANDS	Total	81.30	86.33	75.24
		Rural	78.70	84.14	72.26
		Urban	86.57	90.65	81.47

Some of the important highlights of Census 2001 are given below:

1. The literacy rate in the country has increased to 64.84%, which reflects an overall increase of 12.63%, the fastest decadal growth ever. This is the highest rate since independence.
2. The male literacy rate has increased to 75.26%, which shows an increase of 11.13%. On the other hand, the female literacy of 53.67% has increased at a much faster rate of 14.38%.
3. The male-female literacy gap has reduced from 24.84% in 1991 to 21.59% in 2001. Mizoram has the smallest gap (3.97%) followed by Kerala (6.52%) and Meghalaya (5.82%).
4. All States and Union Territories without exception have shown increase in literacy rates during 1991-2001.
5. In all the States and Union Territories the male literacy rate except Bihar (59.68%) is now over 60%.

6. For the first time since independence there has been a decline in the absolute number of illiterates during the decade. In the previous decades, there has been a continuous increase in the number of illiterates, despite the increase in the literacy rates, but now for the first time the total number of illiterates has come down by 24.77 million.
7. The number of literate persons has increased to 560.68 million in 2001 thus adding an additional 201.40 million literates in the country.
8. Rajasthan has recorded the highest increase i.e. 21.86% in the literacy rate among the States/UTs of India. Literacy rate of Rajasthan in 7+ populations in 1991 was 38.55% which has increased to 60.41% in 2001.
9. The state also recorded very good increase in the female literacy. It was 20.44% in 1991, which has increased to 43.85% in 2001.
10. The female literacy rate of Chhattisgarh in 7+ populations in 1991 was 27.52% which has increased to 51.85% in 2001.Thus the rise in female literacy rate in Chhattisgarh has been to the extent of 24.33%, which is the highest among all the States/UTs of the country.
11. Madhya Pradesh also recorded a good increase in female literacy rate i.e. 20.94%. In 1991 the literacy rate of females was 29.35%, which has increased to 50.29% in 2001.

STATE GROUPINGS

On the basis of literacy rate, State/UTs can be grouped as under:

1. High Literacy Rate (80% and above) — Kerala (90.86%), Mizoram (88.80%), Lakshadweep (86.66%), Goa (82.01%), Chandigarh (81.94%), Delhi (81.67%), A & N Islands (81.30%) and Pondicherry (81.24%).

2. Literacy Rate above national average (64.8%) and below 80% — Daman & Diu (78.18%), Maharashtra (76.88%), Himachal Pradesh (76.48%), Tamil Nadu (73.45%), Tripura (73.19%), Uttaranchal (71.62%), Manipur (70.53%), Punjab (69.65%), Gujarat (69.14%), Sikkim (68.81%), West Bengal (68.64%), Haryana (67.91%), Karnataka (66.64%) and Nagaland (66.59%).
3. Literacy Rate below national average (64.8%) — Chhattisgarh (64.66%), Madhya Pradesh (63.74%), Assam (63.25%), Orissa (63.08%), Meghalaya (62.56%), Andhra Pradesh (60.47%), Rajasthan (60.41%), Dadra & Nagar Haveli (57.63%), Uttar Pradesh (56.27%), Jammu & Kashmir (55.52%), Arunachal Pradesh (54.34%), Jharkhand (53.56%) and Bihar (47.00%).

Rural-Urban Gap (Literates) - Census 2001

(in million)

	Persons	**Male**	**Female**
All Areas	560.68 (64.8%)	336.53 (75.3%)	224.15 (53.7%)
Rural Areas	361.87 (58.7%)	223.55 (70.7%)	138.32 (46.1%)
Urban Areas	199.81 (79.9%)	113.98 (86.3%)	85.83 (72.9%)
SC	75.31 (54.69%)	47.43 (66.64%)	27.88 (41.90%)
ST	32.38 (47.10%)	20.56 (59.17%)	11.82 (34.76%)

ILLITERACY SIZE

1. In terms of the size of illiteracy, eight States, viz. Uttar Pradesh, Bihar, Madhya Pradesh, Rajasthan, Andhra Pradesh, West Bengal, Karnataka and Maharastra had more than 15 million illiterates each and accounted for 69.7 per cent of the illiterate population of the country.

2. The first four of these states – Uttar Pradesh, Bihar, Madhya Pradesh and Rajasthan are in Hindi belt and have 42.76% illiterates.
3. Number of non-literates in these States – Uttar Pradesh (58.85 million), Bihar (35.08 million), Rajasthan (18.15 million) and Madhya Pradesh (17.97 million).
4. In Bihar the number of illiterates increased from 31.98 million in 1991 to 35.08 million in 2001.
5. Jharkhand and Chhattisgarh have 10.21 million and 6.10 million illiterates in 2001.
6. It means that 48.12% of the non-literates reside in these six Hindi-speaking States.
7. Other States having more than 10 million illiterates are: Orissa (11.61 million), Gujarat (13.31 million) and Tamil Nadu (14.65 million).

Total Population and Literacy in 15-35 age-group (Census 2001)

As per Census 2001, the total population of India in 15-35 age-group is 347.67 million, out of which 179.18 million were males and 168.49 million were females. The number of non-literates in this age-group was 100.74 million, out of which 66.78 million were females and 33.96 million were males.

Total Population in 15-35 age-group

		TOTAL		
	Age-group	**Persons**	**Males**	**Females**
1	**2**	**3**	**4**	**5**
INDIA				
	15-19	100,215,890	53,939,991	46,275,899
	20-24	89,764,132	46,321,150	43,442,982
	25-29	83,422,393	41,557,546	41,864,847
	30-34	74,274,044	37,361,916	36,912,128
	15-35	347,676,459	179,180,603	168,495,856

Literate Population in 15-35 Age-group

Age-group	Total	Males	Females
15-19	79,462,115	45,837,429	33,624,686
20-24	65,731,454	38,574,667	27,156,787
25-29	55,931,949	32,863,958	23,067,991
30-34	45,813,001	27,948,542	17,864,459
15-35	246,938,519	145,224,596	101,713,923
Literacy Rate	71.03%	81.04%	60.36%

Non-literate Population in 15-35 Age-group

Age-group	Total	Males	Females
15-19	20,753,775	8,102,562	12,651,213
20-24	24,032,678	7,746,483	16,286,195
25-29	27,490,444	8,693,588	18,796,856
30-34	28,461,043	9,413,374	19,047,669
15-35	100,737,940	33,956,007	66,781,933

FEMALE LITERACY

The Census 2001 final report indicates that India has made significant progress in the field of literacy during the decade and since the 1991 census. The literacy rate as per 2001 census is 64.84% as against 52.21% in 1991, whereas the female literacy had increased by 14.4 percentage points i.e. from 39.3% in 1991 to 53.7% in 2001. Out of 864.79 million people in 7+ age group, 560.68 million are now literate out of which 224.15 million are women. Three-fourths of the male population and more than half of the female population are literate. The trends in literacy rate since 1951 are given below:

It is noticed that the female literacy rate during the period 1991-2001 increased by 14.38% whereas male literacy rose only by 11.13%.

The salient points relating to female literacy are :

- The gap in male-female literacy rates has decreased from 24.8 percentage points in 1991 to 21.6 percentage points in 2001.

Literacy Rates in India (1951-2001)

Census Year	Persons	Male	Female	Male-female gap in literacy rate
1951	18.33	27.16	8.86	18.30
1961	28.30	40.40	15.35	25.05
1971	34.45	45.96	21.97	23.98
1981	43.57	56.38	29.76	26.62
1991	52.21	64.13	39.29	24.84
2001	64.84	75.26	53.67	21.59

- Kerala registered highest female literacy rate at 87.72% while Bihar registered the lowest at 33.12%.
- For the first time there is a decline in absolute number of non-literates. The number of illiterates has reduced from 328 million in 1991 to 304 million in 2001.
- During 1991-2001, the population in 7+age group increased by 171.6 million while 203.6 million additional persons became literate during that period.
- Out of 864.79 million people above the age of 7 years, 560.68 million are now literate.
- All the States and Union territories without exception have shown increase in literacy rates during 1991-2001.
- Kerala continues to have the highest literacy rate of 90.86% in the country with 94.24% literacy rates for males and 87.72% for females.
- Bihar registered a minimum increase of 8.52 percentage points from 38.48% to 47.00%.

STATUS OF LITERACY AMONG SCS AND STS

As per the 2001 Census, the literacy rate of Scheduled Castes population aged 7 years and above was 54.69 per cent. The male and female literacy rate being 66.64 per cent and 41.90 per cent. The literacy rate of Scheduled Caste has increased from 37.41% in 1991 to 54.69% in 2001 (an increase of 17.28%). The increase in overall literacy rate of the country for all persons is 12.63%, whereas increase in literacy rate of Scheduled Caste during the decade is 17.28%. There are 62.4 million SC illiterates out of which 62% (38.7 million) are females. About 47.5 million SC illiterates (76.1%) are residing in the following eight states: Uttar Pradesh (15 million), Bihar (7.2 million), West Bengal (6.4 million), Andhra Pradesh (4.9 million), Rajasthan (3.7 million), Karnataka (3.4 million), Madhya Pradesh (3.1 million) and Tamil Nadu (3.8 million). About 1/3rd of the Scheduled Caste illiterates were residing in Hindi speaking low literacy states of Uttar Pradesh, Bihar, Rajasthan and Madhya Pradesh.

The literacy rate of Schedule Tribes has increased by 17.50% in 2001 (47.10%) from 29.60% in 1991. The increase in overall literacy rate of the country for all persons is 12.63%, whereas increase in literacy rate of Scheduled Tribe during the decade is 17.50%. The male and female literacy rates being 59.17% and 34.76% respectively. The increase in ST female literacy rate increased by 16.57 per cent in a decade. There are 36.4 million ST illiterates in India out of which 21.2 million being female forming 61 per cent of the total ST illiterates. The following are the states having more than 3 million Scheduled Tribe illiterates population: Madhya Pradesh (5.7 million), Orissa (4.2 million), Chhattisgarh (3.8 million), Jharkhand (3.4 million), Gujarat (3.2 million), Maharashtra (3.1 million) and Rajasthan (3.1 million). The number of Scheduled Tribes illiterates in these seven states was 26.5 million, which is 73 per cent of the total Scheduled Tribe illiterates in the country.

Bihar is the state having lowest female Scheduled Castes and Scheduled Tribes literacy rate i.e. 15.58 per cent and 15.54 per cent respectively.

ANALYSIS OF THE NSSO SAMPLE SURVEY DATA ON LITERACY

Apart from census conducted every ten years by the Registrar General and Census Commissioner of India.

National Sample Survey Organisation (NSSO) also conducts all India household sample surveys on Consumer Expenditure and Employment and Unemployment. It takes samples of about 40,000 households (small sample) each year and a sample of about 1,20,000 households (large sample) every five years. These reports also collect some data on literacy.

The report on the basis of 61st round (2004-05) provides data on literacy rates of age group 7 and above at All India level is now available. Literacy rates for the country as revealed by this report is as under:

Area	**61st Round (2004-2005)* July 2004-June 2005**
All Areas	
Persons	67.3
Male	77.0
Female	57.0
Rural Areas	
Persons	61.9
Male	72.7
Female	50.6
Urban Areas	
Persons	82.7
Male	88.8
Female	75.9
Source : Derived from Table 2 of the report	

NATIONAL LITERACY MISSION

The National Literacy Mission (NLM) was launched on 5th May 1988 by late Prime Minsiter Shri Rajiv Gandhi.

The initial experiment of NLM with the campaign mode was first seen in Kottayam city of Kerala. Here the District Collector, by mobilizing 200 volunteers from the local university and forging links with 2000 non-literates in the 6–60 age group, succeeded in making them fully literate within three months.

But, the real breakthrough came with an experiment in mass literacy campaign initiated in 1989 and successfully completed in 1990 in Ernakulam district in Kerala. The campaign for total literacy here saw fusion between the district administrations headed by its Collector, volunteer groups, social activists and others, and was spearheaded by the Kerala Shastra Sahita Parishad (KSSP). Ernakulam achieved this objective on 4th February 1990 and along with it, the unique distinction of being the first district in the country to become 'fully' literate.

The principal shift in strategy adopted in the Ernakulam experiment was a change to a well-coordinated, comprehensive and identifiable initiative. It also marked a change by altering the social context in order to generate demand for the progamme and further to sustain it. It established the feasibility of mass-based, community-based, campaign approach with the objective of generating environment building and demand for literacy followed by literacy instruction. The subsequent adoption of the campaign has taken firm root and has given rise to the Total Literacy Campaign (TLC) approach. Drawing inspiration from the success achieved in Ernakulam, entire Kerala, Goa an UT of Puducherry and several districts in Karnataka, Andhra Pradesh and West Bengal took up the challenge for achieving total literacy in a given time frame. These TLCs had a snowballing effect and campaigns were launched in quick succession all over the country.

Literacy, as enunciated in NLM is not an end in itself but has to be an active and potent instrument of change ensuring achievement of these social objectives and creation of a learning society. The acquisition of functional literacy results in empowerment and a definite improvement in the quality of life.

The Mission objective was to impart functional literacy to 80 million illiterate persons in 15-35 age group - 30 million by 1990 and additional 50 million by 1995. However, now the goal of the Mission is to attain a sustainable threshold literacy rate of 75 per cent by 2007.

National Literacy Mission eventually aims at ensuring that the Total Literacy Campaigns (TLC) and their sequel, the Post-Literacy Programme (PLP), successfully move on to Continuing Education (CE), which provides a life-long learning and also responsible for the creation of a learning society.

The literacy campaigns was one of the biggest movements in the world for eradicating illiteracy. It involved more than 15 million volunteers purely on a voluntary basis. Although the literacy campaigns are being implemented with varying degrees of success, remarkable progress was achieved on several fronts. The campaign was also responsible in the movements on the social evils like anti liquor, dowry system, child marriage and thrift and credit. It also created a conducive environment in reducing the drop out rate of children from school, colossal enrolment of children in the primary schools and success of immunization campaigns.

The mass literacy campaigns and the consequent awakening and recognition of the value of education among the general public has led to a strong demand for universalizing primary education. In several TLC districts such Hoogly in West Bengal, admission figures registered a sharp increase and the over 30 per cent upward swing was attributed to the impact of the TLC in the district.

The literacy movement created awareness regarding the civic rights and played an active role in the participation of public in democratic system. Through this movement, a large number of literacy volunteers specially women, neo-literates and the functionaries were elected as a people representatives in the panchyatiraj institutions.

Some of the significant ways in which the literacy campaigns contributed to the promotion of female literacy and women empowerment are: heightened social awareness, increase in school enrolment, increase in self confidence and personality development, gender equity and women's empowerment, status in the family, educational equality, women as entrepreneurs, house hold saving and access to credit and health and hygiene.

PROGRAMMES UNDER NATIONAL LITERACY MISSION

Literacy Campaigns/Post Literacy Programme: The Total Literacy Campaign is the principal strategy of National Literacy Mission Campaign for eradication of illiteracy. The TLCs have certain positive features, which make them unique and distinguish them from other government programmes. These campaigns are area-specific, time-bound, participative, cost-effective and outcome-oriented.

These are implemented through Zilla Saksharata Samities (ZSS) (district-level literacy committees) as independent and autonomous bodies, having due representation of all sections of society. The ZSS is headed by District Collector/Magistrate. The campaign approach to literacy is characterized by large-scale mobilization through a multi-faceted communication strategy. The survey undertaken at the grass-root level also serves as a tool of planning, mobilization and environment building. The management information system in a campaign is based on the twin principles of participation and correction. Apart from imparting functional literacy, TLC also disseminates a 'basket' of other socially relevant messages such as enrolment and retention of children in schools, immunization, propagation of small family norms, women's equality and empowerment, peace and communal harmony etc.

These literacy campaigns generated a demand for primary education, which has been reflected by rapidly rising enrolment ratio in schools. Consequently, the number of non-literates entering 15-35 age group has been declining. At this stage it is, therefore, necessary to ensure that neo-literates do not relapse into illiteracy and also acquire vocational skills.

The basic literacy skills acquired by millions of non-literates are at best fragile. There is a greater possibility of neo-literates regressing into partial or total illiteracy unless special efforts are continued to consolidate, sustain and possibly enhance their literacy levels. The first phase of basic literacy instruction and the second phase of consolidation, remediation and skill up-gradation (Post Literacy Programme) are now being treated as one integrated project, to ensure smooth progression from one stage to another to achieve continuity, efficiency and convergence. The National Literacy Mission aims at ensuring that the Total Literacy Campaigns and the Post-literacy Programmes successfully move on to Continuing Education, which provide life-long learning.

The TLC and PLP are funded on the basis of a per learner cost. This can range from Rs. 90-180 in respect of TLC and Rs. 90-130 for PLP projects. The duration of TLC is 12 to 18 months, out of which half is devoted to preparations and half to actual teaching/learning activities. The duration of PLP is one year. The total cost of the project is shared between the Central and State Governments for in the ratio of 2:1 respectively for general districts and 4:1 respectively for tribal districts.

The literacy skills are imparted to the beneficiaries in their local dialect, as far as possible. NLM prepares the teaching learning material after taking into account the local needs and the specific requirements of the clientele group. Keeping in view the totally different socio-economic and cultural environment of the tribals, it has been the endeavour of the NLM to prepare the primers suited to the specific requirements of the tribal community in their own tribal language or dialect or the spoken language.

Accelerated Female Literacy Programme: As per Census, 2001, 47 districts in the country had a female literacy rate below 30%. Hence, dealing with low female literacy was of immense concern to the National Literacy Mission and it was decided to target the 47 low female literacy districts for improvement. As most of these districts are concentrated in the States of Uttar Pradesh, Bihar, Orissa and Jharkhand, special innovative programmes were taken up in these districts for promoting female literacy.

A special project 'Accelerated Female Literacy Projects (AFLP)' was launched to raise the female literacy rate of the 8 districts of Uttar Pradesh to cover 25.00 lakhs illiterate women in 15 to 35 age group. The districts are Maharajganj, Siddharathnagar, Balrampur, Gonda, Shravasti, Bahraich, Rampur and Badayun. The programme was implemented through 97 NGOs.

Female literacy programme in the State of Bihar was implemented in 13 low female literacy districts in the Ist phase to cover 24.03 lakhs women learners in 15-35 age group. These districts were West Champaran, East Champaran, Sheohar, Sitamarhi, Supaul, Araria, Kishanganj, Purnia, Madhepura, Saharsa, Khagaria, Banka and Jamui. The projects were implemented under the aegis of Zilla Saksharata Samiti of respective districts with the active involvement of Panchayati Raj functionaries, women volunteer teachers and women Self Help Groups. The special female literacy programme was implemented by the Zilla Saksharata Samitis in the districts along with ongoing TLC, PLP programmes already sanctioned by NLM.

Nine districts in Orissa, having low female literacy rates, were covered under Special Project for Accelerated Female Literacy Programme. These districts are Koraput, Nabrangpur, Malkangiri, Rayagada, Kalahandi, Gajapati, Sonepur, Bolangir and Naupada.

A special female literacy programme was implemented in 5 low female literacy districts of Jharkhand. These districts are Pakur, Garhwa, Sahibganj, Giridih and Godda. The programme was implemented under the aegis of Zilla Saksharata Samities of respective districts with the active involvement of Panchayati Raj Institutions/women social workers etc.

Although the Total Literacy Campaigns took the form of a mass movement and spread throughout the country, in many cases a number of campaigns stagnated due to natural calamities, lack of political will, frequent transfer of Collectors, etc. Despite success of literacy phase, there were still pockets of residual illiteracy.

In these areas, Projects for Residual Illiteracy (PRIs) were taken after the conclusion of TLCs to cover the remaining illiterates. PRIs have so far been taken up in 9 districts of Rajasthan, 10 districts of Andhra Pradesh, 7 districts of Bihar, 14 districts of Karnataka and 3 districts of Tripura. PRIs were also sanctioned in 12 districts of Madhya Pradesh and 8 districts of West Bengal.

Special literacy drive in 150 districts: The Council of the National Literacy Mission Authority in its 8th meeting held on 11.4.2005 took stock of the progress made in promoting literacy in the country and was of the view that a renewed focus and revitalization of the National Literacy Mission was needed to reach the target of 75% literacy by 2007. The Council, based on 2001 census literacy data, decided to take up a special literacy drive in 150 districts, which have the lowest literacy rates in the country. These 150 districts are mainly in the States of Uttar Pradesh, Bihar, Jharkhand, Rajasthan, Madhya Pradesh, Chhattisgarh and Orissa. The special drive for reduction of the residual illiteracy aims to cover nearly 36 million illiterates between 2005-07. So far, 134 districts in the States of Arunachal Pradesh (7), Andhra Pradesh (8), Bihar (26), Chhattisgarh (4), Jammu & Kashmir (8), Rajasthan (9), Jharkhand (12), Karnataka (2), Madhya Pradesh (9), Meghalaya (3), Nagaland (2), Orissa (10), Punjab (1), Uttar Pradesh (24) and West Bengal (4) have been covered under the Special Literacy drive.

Continuing Education: The Continuing Education Scheme provides a learning continuum to the efforts of Total Literacy and Post Literacy Programmes in the country. The main thrust is on providing further learning opportunities to neo-literates by setting up of Continuing Education

Centres (CECs) which provide area-specific, need-based opportunities for basic literacy, upgradation of literacy skills, pursuit of alternative educational programmes, vocational skills and also promote social and occupational development. The scheme also undertakes a number of important programmes such as Equivalency programme, facilitating the participants to acquire or upgrade their vocational skills and take up income-generating activities; Quality of life improvement programme to equip learners and the community with essential knowledge, attitude, values and skills to raise their standards of living; and Individual interest promotion programme providing opportunities for learners to participate and learn about their individually chosen social, health, physical, cultural, and artistic interests.

Under the scheme the main thrust is given to setting up of Continuing Education Centre (CEC) which will function as a focal point for providing learning opportunities such as library, reading room, learning centre, training centre, information centre, charcha mandal, development centre, cultural centre, sports centre and other individual interest promotion programme centre. One CEC is set up for a population of 2000 to 2500. For a group of about 10-15 CECs, there is a Nodal CEC, which monitors and oversees the activities of those cluster of CECs. Besides the provisions of setting up of CECs, the scheme of Continuing Education also provides the opportunities to undertake diverse activities involving alternative and innovative approaches to cater to the needs of the learners. Taking into account local conditions and the resources available, various target specific activities such as Equivalency Programmes (EPs), Quality of Life Improvement Programmes (QLIPs), Income Generating Programmes (AGPs) and Individual Interest Promotion Programmes (IIPPs) could be organized for specific groups of beneficiaries.

The programmes of Continuing Education are being implemented under the aegis of Zilla Saksharata Samitis.

ZSSs along with district, block and gram panchayat level committees are responsible to oversee the programme in the entire district.

Each CEC will be annually provided assistance of Rs. 25,000/- as recurring and non-recurring grant, and nodal CEC Rs. 45,000/- as recurring and non-recurring grant with an additional provision of house rent for few selected centres where no government or community building is available to run the centre. In the revised scheme a provision of Assistant Prerak has been made who will be primarily responsible for conducting literacy classes during continuing education programme.

The scheme envisages 100 per cent assistance to the States for the first three years of the implementation. The State Governments are required to share 50 per cent of the expenditure during the 4th and 5th year of the project, and thereafter take over the total responsibility for the programme.

Involvement of NGOs: The National Literacy Mission (NLM) fully recognizes the vast potential of NGOs in furthering its objectives and has taken measures to strengthen its partnership with NGOs and has assigned them an active promotional role in the literacy movement. Apart from imparting literacy, the NGOs provide academic and technical resource support through experimental and innovative programmes and also conducting evaluation and impact studies; organization of workshops, seminars, etc.

State Resource Centres: The scheme of establishing State Resource Centres at State level was formulated by the then Ministry of Education in 1976 with the objective of providing technical and resource support to the adult education programme on the recommendation of Standing Committee of the CABE.

The State Resource Centres function under the aegis of Non Government Organizations (NGOs) or Universities. Beginning with 14 State Resource Centres in 1980s the number has gone up to 26. These State Resource Centres provide technical and academic resource support to the literacy programmes in the country.

The role and functions of State Resource Centres have expanded over the years. Initially, focus of the State Resource Centres was on Non-Formal Education (NFE) of the drop-out children and un-enrolled youth, after the launching of National Adult Education Programme (NAEP) in 1978, the State Resource Centres were required to concentrate on the eradication of illiteracy among 15-35 age-group by organizing training programmes and production of teaching/ learning material for Adult Education. All State Resource Centres have Population and Development Education Units (PDE). PDE units also prepare teaching/learning materials publicity material and organize training programmes for literacy functionaries and NGOs on the Population and Development Education including HIV/AIDS themes.

Main functions of State Resource Centres:

1. Development of teaching/learning and training materials for literacy programmes.
2. Production and dissemination (including translation) of literature for adult education.
3. Training literacy functionaries.
4. Undertaking motivational and environment building activities for adult education.
5. Multi media works.
6. Running of field programmes.
7. Action research, evaluation and monitoring of literacy projects.
8. Undertaking innovative projects to identify future need of literacy programmes.

Some of the SRCs have taken up several innovative projects, which are pioneering. For example, SRC, Kolkata has initiated an Action Research Project on Life Skills Education for the benefit of commercial sex workers and their adolescent girls. In addition, they are also counselling on HIV/AIDS.SRC, Tamil Nadu is providing resource support, in collaboration with Chennai Municipal Corporation for setting up Special Schools for street children so that they are re-enrolled in formal schools. These special schools also help in identifying individual talents in these children and provide facilities for further nurturing their talents either in sports, arts or academics. SRC, Kerala in collaboration with the Kerala Federation of the Blind has converted the basic literacy primer to the Braille letter for the benefit of visually imparted adult illiterate population. This Braille Literacy Programme is being taken up in the Mallapuram Panchayat for 300 blind persons and the centres are being run under the supervision of the Nodal Preraks of the Continuing Education Centres.

Jan Shikshan Sansthan: The scheme of Jan Shikshan Sansthan (JSS) is a unique scheme crafted by the Government of India. JSSs are institutes of People's Education focusing on the poor, the illiterates, the neo-literates, the under-privileged and the un-reached. The Jan Shikshan Sansthans are unique in that they do not provide just skill development, but link literacy with vocational skills and provide large doses of Life Enrichment Education (LEE) to the people. They do not work in isolation but aim for convergence with other stakeholders in society. It is their endeavour to shape their beneficiaries into self-reliant and self-assured employees and entrepreneurs.

The Jan Shikshan Sansthans are unique also because they offer quality vocational skills and technical knowledge at a very low cost. Their doors are open to everyone and they reach out to their clientele groups by setting up sub centres in the heart of the slum or in remote rural areas. They are different from other vocational training institutions as they offer quality vocational skills and technical knowledge at such a low cost; provide need based and literacy-linked vocational training in most courses without insisting on age limit or prior educational qualifications; reach out to the clientele in their areas unlike other institutions which the clientele has to access whether near or far; offer a multi-faceted skill-knowledge-awareness enhancement and outlook formation trainings and inputs and empowerment-oriented interventions in respect of social, economic and health status improvement of women and adolescent girls.

The scheme of Jan Shikshan Sansthan (JSS) was initially launched in 1967 as Shramik Vidyapeeth, a polyvalent or multi-faceted adult education institution, aimed at improving the vocational skills and quality of life of the industrial workers and their family members as well as those persons who had been migrating from rural to urban settings.

The scheme of Shramik Vidyapeeth was renamed as Jan Shikshan Sansthan in April 2000.Along with the change in its name came the change in its focus. A scheme that was meant for the industrial workers and their families was expanded both in terms of its clientele and focus and was extended to the rural areas. There was logic for its expansion. Total Literacy Campaigns, launched after the setting up of the National Literacy Mission in 1988, had transformed the literacy landscape of the country and created an army of neo-literates who having realized the power of the written word, now wanted to use it to improve their livelihoods through skill development. The post-literacy programme had given a few of them the taste of vocational skills but the continuing education programme promised to extend it to many more beneficiaries. That became the rationale of setting up more Jan Shikshan Sansthans, to match the needs of the districts. Today, there 221 Jan Shikshan Sansthans in the country and they are expected to act as district level resource support agencies especially in regard to organization of vocational training and skill development programmes for the neo-literates and other target groups of the continuing education programme. The current aim is that the JSSs should progressively move towards having 50% of their beneficiaries from amongst the neo-literates. The state-wise list of JSSs established so far is given below:

Sl. No.	STATE/UT	Number of JSSs
1	ANDHRA PRADESH	12
2	ARUNACHAL PRADESH	1
3	ASSAM	3
4	BIHAR	9
5	CHHATTISGARH	3
6	DELHI	3
7	GOA	1
8	GUJARAT	8
9	HARYANA	6
10	JAMMU & KASHMIR	2
11	JHARKHAND	5
12	KARNATAKA	10
13	KERALA	11
14	MADHYA PRADESH	27
15	MAHARASHTRA	18
16	MANIPUR	3
17	MIZORAM	1
18	NAGALAND	1
19	ORISSA	15
20	PUNJAB	2
21	RAJASTHAN	6
22	TAMILNADU	10
23	TRIPURA	1
24	UTTARAKHAND	6
25	UTTAR PRADESH	47
26	WEST BENGAL	9
27	CHANDIGARH	1
	TOTAL	**221**

The objectives of JSS were redefined in the context of the literacy movement which was graduating rapidly into Post-Literacy (PL) and Continuing Education (CE) phases, with vocational and life skill up-gradation as a part of their agenda. The enhanced role of the JSS included the following:

(i) impact vocational skills, life skills and technical knowledge to neo-literates and their trainees and raise their efficiency and increase their productive ability;

(ii) provide academic and technical resource support to Zila Saksharta Samiti (ZSS), including training its Resource Persons, Master Trainers and Preraks, to take up vocational and skill development programmes primarily for neoliterates;

(iii) serve as Nodal Continuing Education Centre (NCEC) and also to manage, coordinate, supervise and monitor 10-20 CECs, as envisaged in the Scheme of Continuing Education Programme;

(iv) organize equivalency programmes for its beneficiaries through National and State Open Schools;

(v) through Life Enrichment Education (LEE), wide the knowledge and understanding of the social, economic and political systems among its beneficiaries in order to create a critical awareness about the environment;

(vi) promote national goals such as secularism, national integration, women's equality, protection and conservation of the environment.

The Jan Shikshan Sansthans offer a large number of vocational training programmes from candle making to computer courses. In the year 2006-07, 17.53 lakh beneficiaries have been covered under various vocational training programmes and other activities.

NLM – AN ASSESSMENT

The literacy campaigns, the dominant strategy of the NLM after the Ernakulum campaign, saw an unprecedented mobilization of the society and community for imparting functional literacy to the non-literates Ernakulum and Kottayam in Kerala, Pudukottai in Tamil Nadu, Nellore and West Godavari in Andhra Pradesh, Birbhum, Burdwan and

Midnapore in West Bengal, Durg in Madhya Pradesh, Ajmer, Jhunjhunu, and Sikar in Rajasthan, Roopnagar in Punjab, Dumka in Jharkhand and Begusarai in Bihar were examples of successful literacy districts. The focus of NLM was not merely the learning of the three R's, but on functional literacy, which included "knowing the causes of one's deprivation and taking steps for their amelioration," and emphasized the values of national integration and small family norms. The literacy rates saw impressive gains on the whole, having risen from 52% in 1991 to 64.8% in 2001, though regional variations and disparities are still a matter of concern.

The mission mode of the early 90's, made way for a programme based approach when the PLPs were sanctioned. While TLCs threw up many interesting and innovative models, unfortunately the Post Literacy Programmes did not. PLP began to be viewed as a transitional phase during which a district was being readied for Continuing Education Programme. The political and administrative will to implement literacy programmes was also reduced in many states of the country. The CECs, were envisaged as centres of lifelong learning, but they functioned merely as reading rooms and recreational centres, where occasionally some residual illiterates were imparted literacy skills. No funds were provided for the target specific programmes viz. the Equivalency, a number of reasons were responsible for the lukewarm response to the Scheme of Continuing Education. This included a extremely low, inadequate budget provision, delay in the operationalization of the CECs by the districts, non-implementation of the target specific programmes viz the equivalency programme, the income generation programme, the quality of life improvement programme and the individual interest promotion programme; inadequate motivation and training of Voluntary Teachers/Preraks, inadequate payment made to literacy functionaries; lack of dedicated functionaries for the adult education programmes; lack of convergence with other developmental programmes, low levels of community participation. The Continuing

Education Programme, in effect, was not able to realize its full potential. These drawbacks/gaps would be addressed in a more focused manner.

In the meanwhile the literacy scenario underwent a sea change. The literacy map of India changed. 95 districts in India are in basic literacy phase, 174 in post literacy phase and 328 in the Continuing Education phase. There are 124 million neo-literates, which have been covered under literacy programmes so far for whom, lifelong opportunity need to be provided. There is also need to amalgamate the three phases of literacy, basic literacy, post-literacy and continuing education into one so that the gains of skill development, quality of life improvement, self reliance and empowerment, the basic tenets of literacy as defined by the NLM are reached to all districts, especially those difficult districts in the Hindi speaking belt which are still in the basic literacy phase.

The NLM has been now focused on achieving a threshold level of 75% literacy by 2007.GOAL 4 of EFA as applicable to literacy aims at achieving a 50% improvement in levels of adult literacy by 2015, especially for women and equitable access to basic and continuing education for all adults. Planning Commission lays down a target of 85% literacy rate to be achieved by the end of the XI Plan.

The growth rate for literacy during the past decade has been 12.63%. While the male literacy has grown by 11.13%, female literacy has grown by 14.38%. In order to achieve a target of 85% overall literacy rate, it is imperative that the rate of growth of male literacy is raised to 1 4% during the XI Plan by changing the strategy and introducing innovations, so that the male literacy grows to 90% by 2011. Female literacy would have to be raised to at least 80% by the end of the Plan period so that the gender gap is minimized to 10%.

The revamped strategy of the NLM includes an integrated comprehensive learning programme called Lifelong Education and Awareness Programme.

GOALS FOR THE XI PLAN

The target for the XI Plan is to achieve 85% literacy by 2012. The target for male literacy is 90% and for female literacy is 80%. The gender gap in literacy is to be reduced to 10% along with bridging of regional, social and gender disparities. The illiterates in the 35+ age-group are also expected to be covered through a computer based self-learning system. New models of continuing education will be developed to reach a much higher level of literacy.

The goals as laid down in the Approach Paper of the Planning Commission would mean that a new age-group (35+) would be added to the target. This would mean a target of covering 259.52 million illiterates during the XI Plan. In addition, there are already 124 million neo-literates whose needs for lifelong learning have to be addressed.

Revised strategy for the XI Plan: The existing schemes of Total Literacy Campaign (TLC), Post Literacy Programme (PLP) and Continuing Educaiton Programme (CEP) have been amalgamated into a single scheme known as 'Adult Education and Skill Development'. The thrust of the programme would be on addressing the learning needs of the illiterates and neo-literates, providing them with opportunities of lifelong learning and skill development, and linking them with issues of rights, governance and livelihoods. The new programme to be launched after amalgamating the TLC, PLP and CE stages is called Lifelong Education and Awareness Programme (LEAP). The main features of the LEAP are:

1. Different types of learning packages and learning programmes to suit the needs of various categories of beneficiaries.
2. Life Skills Education with focus on communication skills, problem solving skills, entrepreneurial skills etc.

3. Inforamtion window on Health, Rural Development, Environment Conservation etc.
4. Target Specific Programme particularly Equivalency Programmes to mainstream the neo-literates and others with the formal system.
5. Rural libraries with focus on neo-literates literature.
6. Awareness Programmes to discuss on issues like RTI, REGP, NRHM, HIV/AIDS etc.

❑❑❑

2

Principles and Modelling of Education and Development

INTRODUCTION

The term "development" denotes *change*, and technically it can be viewed from either a positive or a negative perspective. However, in most cases, development refers to *positive changes*. All societies undergo changes as multidimensional phenomena impact social, economic, and political systems, causing societal actions and reactions. Development is an ongoing strategic process designed to influence changes for positive outcomes. Contrary to erroneous contemporary labels (e.g., developing countries), all societies are developing. The non-industrial, impoverished countries of the world are struggling to deal with problems associated with the lack of modernization or industrialization, whereas the industrialized countries of the world are struggling to deal with problems associated with the *effects* of modernization or industrialization. Most writers refer to development for modernization as a process that is needed by non-industrial countries in Africa, Asia, and Latin America. In North America, development is usually discussed in terms of its application to urban inner cities and rural areas. This selective use of the term obscures and narrows its fullest conceptual scope. Development happens at all geographic and socio-economic strata. An abundance of long-standing community-based organizations found in many middle and upper class communities in the United States is engaged in many facets of development.

Education as the driving force or *sine qua non* for citizen participation in development is undisputed, particularly when education is viewed and positioned as the major component in the strategy for development. Oftentimes the substantive activities of development involving citizens that are "educational" may not explicitly be identified as such. However, an investigation of democratic development schemes across the globe will reveal that education is vital in promoting intelligent citizen participation for community development. Adult education is particularly relevant because it is designed to deliver instruction to the most able agents of community development its adult residents. In very practical terms, it is the adults, rather than the children, who in any development situation stand out as the most important human resource agents to bridge the transition of community reform and transformation. It is their services and participation that are most urgently needed in the planning and execution of development activities. They cannot carry out their roles unless they are sufficiently well informed to select from the many action options open to them.

It should be stressed that at the national, regional, and community levels the aim is not to require a massive number of people in development efforts. Lindeman wrote, "we need not await the tide of numbers: a small group of adults in a single community seriously concerned about the values of creative living is sufficient to alter the quality of the total community process". Education as a prerequisite for development has a growing consensus. The present challenge centers around what form it should take for maximum effectiveness.

COMMUNITY-BASED ADULT EDUCATION

The terms "community-based adult education" and "nonformal education" are used synonymously in this book. They refer to "any organized educational activity outside the established formal system that is intended to serve identifiable learning clientele and learning objectives". In the truly community-based models, control is in the hands of community residents. These models are autonomous educational activities initiated, controlled, and evaluated by a group of local citizens. The community-based program may have links with a formal educational institution, but is not dictated to, or controlled by, the formal agency. Community-based models have proliferated in North America because of the absence of effective public or institutional adult education programs to meet changing community needs. There is a broad range of educational activities based on current community needs that can be impacted by educational intervention. Each community has its own special problems, which sometimes may not be addressed appropriately by national or regional program models. It is the flexibility of nonformal education that allows the customization of the educational intervention. Nonformal education is a practical, rather than an abstract, approach to learning. Compared to formal schooling, nonformal education can be characterized conceptually as being learner-centered, using local resources, and having community-oriented content, horizontal relationships between facilitator and learner, an immediate time focus, and age inclusivity. Even though self-reliance is the hallmark of nonformal education, it does not preclude requests for assistance that are external to the community. Such extra-local agencies may be private and public institutions. However, community organizers must always be aware and concerned about external assistance because of the need to maintain autonomy and control.

The nonindustrial countries of the world have steadily increased the use of nonformal education as a complementary process to formal education. Traditionally, the national emphasis of most of these governments has been on children's education. Expenditures for adult education in Africa and Latin America represent a small fraction of expenditures allocated for youth education. Adult education usually is carried out under sporadic mass literacy campaigns. Given this context, nonformal education is being increasingly viewed as a compatible vehicle through which societal reform and transformation can be accelerated. Some countries are beginning to understand that in the short run, adult education offers a quicker dividend for nation building than does the long-run education of its youth. Adults in societies where the great majority of the population have had little or no education represent a monumental reservoir of people who are unproductive for themselves and their communities. This "unproductiveness" affects all aspects of their lives.

The World Bank investigated the impact of education on health in a large number of mostly nonindustrial countries. The focal point of the studies was the literacy level of adult parents as it affected child nutrition and mortality. The findings in most cases revealed a significant positive relationship between the literacy level of the mother/father and its predictive value on the nutritional and life expectancy status of the child. In many of these countries, parental education is offered through nonformal education approaches.

Nonformal education has a substantial history in most African countries. In the last ten years, the majority of these programs have been devoted to skills training for employment. Thompson classifies skills training in three categories: "pre-employment training for industry, skills upgrading for small businesses, and training for farmers and craftsmen in rural areas".

The community-based adult education concept is continuing to emerge and cannot readily be understood according to any conceptual scheme. It perhaps is similar to the conceptual typology that Brookfield describes as *adult education in the community*. He states, "The distinct features of such practice are that the learners retain control over the direction and execution of their learning, and that assistance is offered only after a period of immersion by the educator in community group activities". Traditionally, the professional field of adult education has largely ignored community-based adult education. The vast majority of professional adult educators are involved in public school adult education, community college and university continuing education, and the fastest growing area (for profit)—*human resource development*. Yet, the trend of increasing nonformal education, particularly in communities in North America, appears to be firmly established as an alternate means of learning for problem solving and action.

Nonformal education has been given little attention by researchers in the West who publish in the traditional literature base of adult education and community development. Studies of nonformal education are more likely found in newspapers, newsletters, and a limited number of monographs. Because of the independent nature of nonformal education conducted by community-based organizations, there is no regional or national reporting station that collects discrete data for multiple analyses of program types, goals, and outcomes.

The best estimate of adult participation in community organizations in the United States was reported in the National Center for Education Statistics report. This report estimated that among churches, synagogues, YMCAs and YWCAs, Red Cross chapters, civic organizations, and social and literary societies, there were approximately 11 million participants. Most of these organizations are the traditional types, which are supportive of community-based education for development, but are not organized specifically to pursue social change at the neighbourhood and community levels. The emerging community-based adult education of today is homegrown organized learning designed to focus on local issues and problems for the express purpose of bringing about reformation and transformation. Because of the private and nonprofit nature of community-based organizations, there is a dearth of research data available to analyze national and regional developments. In some cases they are referred to as adult community schools, learning exchanges, free universities, and block clubs for civic and political education and action. Many are nonformal programs on adult literacy, parenthood, crime-watch, tenant housing control, school-community relations, ethnic/racial history and culture, and hundreds of other learning activities related to local issues and needs. How many such community-based organizations there are in North America is not known.

COMMUNITY DEVELOPMENT

Community development is usually thought about and discussed in purely economic and political terms. The educational dimension is usually underemphasized or implicitly treated. Economic models of community development have often failed because of a narrow bureaucratic focus on capital investment outcomes without consideration of investments for human development. Community development in regard to the human capital theory may also be viewed differently in industrialized countries, compared to non industrialized nations. The degree of these differences is largely determined by the level of local political autonomy that characterizes the country or geographic area. The following definitions reflect perspectives from the United States, Britain, India, and Nigeria.

UNITED STATES

The term "community development" refers to "a social process by which human beings can become more competent to live with and gain some control over local aspects of a frustrating and changing world". Mezirow states, "The community development process is, in essence, a planned and organized effort to assist individuals to acquire the attitudes, skills and concepts required for their democratic participation in the effective solution of as wide a range of community improvement problems as possible in the order of priority determined by their increasing levels of competence". Rubin stresses the goal of empowerment: "Community development involves local empowerment through organized groups of people acting collectively to control decisions, projects, programs and policies that affect them as a community". Many American writers emphasize learning, participation, and action as key components of community development in the United States.

BRITAIN

Community development is a movement designed to promote "better living for the whole community with the active participation and, if possible, on the initiative of the community". Du Sutoy defines community development as part of an overall process of building communities.

It is part of the process which can be distinguished by the following ingredients: self-help; attention paid to peoples' felt needs; attention paid to the social, traditional, and other aspects of the community as a whole. It usually operates in four main fields: adult literacy and basic social education; specialized work among women and youth; self-help construction projects; and extension education in various nation-building fields. It may also concern itself with co-operatives and the stimulation of cottage industry.

In recent years there has been much interest in Britain in increasing the abilities of working-class people through adult education. Lovett describes some efforts to create a functional relationship between adult education and community development among working-class people in Liverpool.

INDIA

Community development is "a method and ideology for promoting the improvement of rural areas of the country on democratic lines and with the active participation of the people". It is initiated and controlled by central government agencies working with village representatives on local problems. Community development in India has focused on literacy since the establishment of the National Literacy Mission in 1988. Its goal is to enable 80 million adults to become functionally literate by 1995. Functional literacy means "achieving self-reliance in literacy and numeracy, becoming aware of the causes of their deprivation and moving towards amelioration of their conditions through organization and participation in the process of development". Community development is viewed as a method by which all the technical services of government can be channelled down to meet and assist the gigantic developing potential power of thousands of organized villages.

NIGERIA

There are many definitions of community development in Nigeria. The one used by most state governments is this: "Community development is the process by which the efforts of the people themselves are united with those of governmental authorities to improve the economic, social and cultural conditions of communities, to integrate these communities in the life of the nation, and to enable them to contribute fully to national progress". Definitions of community development in Nigeria refer to rural and urban settings separately. Integrated rural development refers to government agencies working cooperatively with rural communities to tackle rural development problems in order to improve and increase the per capita income and the welfare of the people. Rural development is also designed to "encourage people to stay in their areas and work the land rather than flocking to cities to swell the number of the unemployed".

Internationally, community development can be viewed in many forms, structures, and levels. National and Regional Development Schemes are more likely to be focused toward economic and political objectives. Increasingly, local development schemes, particularly those in industrialized countries, are more likely to reflect unique local concerns and issues. Local community development has traditionally been initiated by local governments. To some extent these government initiatives have been characterized as being cosmetic and superficial efforts to maintain the societal *status quo* and prevent any real social change for the people at the bottom of society. These beliefs have given rise to the organization and proliferation of locally controlled community development. One of these movements is known as "popular education," which originated in Latin America. Paulo Freire, the father of popular education, advocates a process of "conscientization" as a central philosophy in developing community knowledge and awareness for social transformation. Abernathy argues that popular education faces a political dilemma in that transformation involves destroying traditional hegemonic structures and replacing them with different hegemonic structures, which may also tend to be oppressive. Popular education shares some similarities with community development, which is locally controlled and utilizes nonformal procedures in its educational strategy. Both can be shaped to achieve social reform and transformation.

PROCESS AND TASK ORIENTATIONS

Community development has two basic orientations or dimensions. First is the *process*, which focuses on developing social relationships among community residents. Warren discusses the process orientation of community development and states that it is "a deliberate and sustained attempt to strengthen the horizontal pattern of a community". The process begins when one or more community residents start establishing relationships that lead to a systematic discussion of problems and issues. Usually, one or two individuals in the community assume leadership roles in the facilitation of discussions that identify the most important problems to confront and reason about solutions and planning. These psychosocial interactions are designed to raise consciousness levels to the point where residents begin to view themselves as partners in community development. The process is ongoing; it starts with the identification of rather simple problems and in time proceeds to tackle more complex problems. Increasingly, learning and motivation become important cognitive components of the development process. Schler surmises, "As people learn to discuss, reason and act together to solve commonly defined problems, new identities, meanings, and relationships emerge among community members".

The second dimension is the task orientation. Task goals and accomplishments relate to specific capital and human resource projects (e.g., a playground, supermarket, or health clinic). It may or may not strengthen horizontal ties in the community. Task goals are short-range and conclusive, and they usually represent top-down approaches to community development. Compton and McClusky warn us that highly centralized approaches bring about "*little improvement in the planning and management skills of local people, and little incorporation of the indigenous experience and knowledge in education and development efforts*". However, when the *task* orientation is a direct consequence of *process*, a desired state of compatibility for the two orientations evolves.

The total pursuit of a task may weaken horizontal ties and damage the self-reliant community-building capability of the residents. For example, the local city government of a small town decided to expand the parking lot of a public library located in a low-income neighbourhood. This action came about as a result of demands from an increasing number of middle-class users because of the proximity of the library to their neighbourhood. Residents of the low-income neighbourhood were consulted only after the architect had drawn plans and scheduled a public hearing. From the task perspective, community development occurred because the goal was to expand the parking capacity of the library. From the process perspective, community development may not have occurred. Residents from the low-income neighbourhood had no input at the early stages of the proposal. Will they agree that the local quality of life will be enhanced by this action? If not, will they be able to block this action? An ultimate negative decision by public officials to proceed without local input to expand the parking lot will likely serve to weaken local confidence and horizontal ties. When this happens, the two orientations of community development are in conflict.

In the long run, process probably takes precedence over task. Process stresses endogenous development, which Perroux summarizes as a locally initiated plan which is based on the identification of potential human resources, dividing responsibilities between self-reliance and outside collaboration, and establishing permanent communication between a downward and upward flow of information. Many facets of community development are drawn from multidisciplinary sources. Some discussion of the major disciplines involved is warranted.

INTERDISCIPLINARY NATURE

There exists no single theory of community development as an academic discipline. Rather, community development is multidisciplinary and borrows from many scientific fields, mainly the social sciences. It uses a smorgasbord application of the appropriate conceptual elements to bring about desired social change. Moreover, since community development is heavily engaged in politics, leadership, group dynamics, learning, and social change, it draws from disciplines such as political science, sociology, social psychology, social work, and education.

Community development is both an emerging field of study and a field of practice. What distinguishes it as a field of study is that students seek to explore social systems for the purpose of gaining insights and understandings about human behaviour in the context of community living. Community research is the lifeline for theory building and hypothesis testing. **Blakely** writes that "*the focus of research output in community development is designed to discover new applications of intervention strategies in government and social institutions that will improve the quality of community life*". What distinguishes community development as a field of practice is that it is premised on two assumptions. First, people have the ability to analyze the conditions of their lives, and they have the capability and determination to plan together to improve the quality of community life. A second assumption is based on the belief that development should start at the grass-roots level and that people bonding together can learn and apply their knowledge and skill to resolving problems related to the betterment of the community.

Biddle and Biddle provide a discussion of three behavioural scientific fields that appear to be important to community development sociology, anthropology, and social psychology. Traditionally, sociologists have tended to focus on the community as a social structure, absent any real humanistic or ethical considerations. This involves viewing the community through basic sociological concepts such as stratification, mobility, social structure, organizational behaviour, class and race subdivisions, and hierarchies of power. Berstein suggests that sociology can be more useful in adult education by exploring ways in which society classifies, transmits, and analyzes knowledge. Community development advocates in North America, Asia, and Africa can learn much from studies of counter hegemonic worker movements in Europe. Great strides have been made to improve the use of anthropological techniques in community development. First was the movement from "uninvolved observer" to "participant observer." This was due to the belief that an "outsider" would never be able to understand what was occurring with the people for example, why people did what they did and how they felt about it. A further improvement of the technique is mentioned by Biddle and Biddle in which the anthropologist becomes active in the process, involved in and encouraging "action" changes by recording and evaluating the progress of community development. If the emphasis of sociology is on the social structure, and that of anthropology is on the process, then only social psychology gives full attention to people. In social psychology, the emphasis is on group dynamics and the human personality as a contributor to planned development for the common good.

INSTITUTIONAL VS. COMMUNITY-BASED DEVELOPMENT

In most countries, citizen groups and other community-based mediating units predate the establishment and growth of government public service agencies. Over the years, the two sectors have been able to form partnerships for community action. Some of the ventures have been successful because of the compatibility of the goals and values of the two forces. Today, most public service agencies have some level of citizen involvement, which is designed to assist and provide support for decision-making relative to a government program. However, *citizen involvement* is not the same as *citizen action*. According to **Langton**, *citizen involvement in the United States is legislatively mandated, and almost all major government programs at the state and federal* *levels contain this requirement.* Citizen action is usually performed through a community based organization. It is a bottom-up effort initiated by citizens to deliver non-formal education and an assortment of many services, and to monitor and lobby government officials, industry, and others to influence change. Substantial reform in government and industry in North America has been made as a result of effective citizen action.

At the community and neighbourhood levels each sector has had a different impact in meeting the needs of residents. It is clear that only big government can resolve massive problems faced by many communities. Yet, there are residual problems unique to given communities that receive no government response, or an ineffective response, or too little too late. As a result of these mixed patterns of government action, and in the spirit of community self-reliance, community-based organizations have continued to emerge and flourish.

However, there are stark differences as to how each sector responds to community problem solving. Each has its own set of strengths and weaknesses. Government agencies command vast amounts of material and personnel resources. They employ professionals who represent a cross-section of specialties. They can mobilize great quantities of resources and services for large populations. Government programs also reflect many limitations. Officials must follow policy and regulations that may not be appropriate for all situations requiring intervention.

Administrators may assume responsibility for running agencies without having reliable information or the time to make good decisions. Community-based organizations, composed frequently of people residing in the community, are aroused through personal experiences and have a vested interest in the solving of unmet needs of the community. In the words of **Fingeret** in addressing adult literacy programs, "*Community-oriented organizations are committed to empowerment, or increasing the ability of persons and groups* *to control their lives*". However, most community-based organizations lack sufficient levels of material and personnel resources. They must raise money in the community and seek grants from government and private foundations.

Five common problems that plague community organizations are cited by Mico: "1. vague purpose; 2. inadequate funds; 3. inability to work together effectively; 4. inability to plan activities and solve problems; and 5. unwillingness to cooperate with other community based organizations". Yet in the face of these serious problems many organizations are able to survive and even expand. Community-based organizations often link with public agencies for different reasons. They demand control of their operation and even fight to control component programs that are government funded.

In recent years many social activists have become advocates for increasing community control of government programs. **Hallman** argues that there is a need for an overall strategy and states, "*A thorough going strategy of community control will require us to rethink some of the basic premises that have come to dominate administrative theory*".

SOCIAL LEARNING

If *learning* is an under girding force that drives community development, which learning theories appear to be important? Learning is generally defined as a change in behaviour. According to **Roberts**, "*in community development we are therefore concerned with individual learning that brings about, or is required for, behaviour whose effects will be a change in social relationships*". The ideas of Ivan Illich and Paulo Freire have been most influential in promoting adult learning theories for non-formal education. This is not to discount Thorndike, Rogers, Skinner, Bruner, and Knowles for their outstanding contributions to learning theory development. The importance of adult learning theory is particularly useful for community facilitators who will assist in the design of non-formal education. Basic assumptions about how adults learn provide the foundation for the program-designing process.

Learning is directly related to fulfilling social needs. As environmental forces change, former social learning skills become obsolete. New social skills must be learned to satisfy old needs. This requires learning new methods of fulfilling fundamental needs in relation to Maslow hierarchy, in which survival needs come first. Individuals must learn new skills that can satisfy social needs in a dynamic society.

Social learning is primarily associated with adults as it relates to their social role responsibilities. Most adults' daily life cycles are conducted in the social domain. Fundamentally, adults are involved in an endless pursuit of activities and tasks in order to provide food, clothing, shelter, transportation, and other basic necessities for themselves and their families. Social learning is not synonymous with education in the sense that it can become codified and amenable to discrete topics, objectives, and predictable outcomes. Thomas discusses social learning from the central role of being a *citizen*. He contends that the citizen role is pivotal and inclusive in the social domain, involving, for example, "the economic roles of entrepreneur or worker; the social roles of parent, sibling and friend; and the political roles of government leader or elected representative, to name but a few". Generally, social learning is connected to education, but is beyond formal learning. Social learning is acquired through experiential encounters and efforts to adjust and accommodate dynamic societal phenomena. Social learning is particularly important to educational aspects of community development. Since social learning tends to include both informal and nonformal transactions, it enables citizens to develop critical thinking skills. Social learning and community development take place in the naturalistic setting of the community. There is a point of convergence between social learning within a broad context and community learning in a more restricted context. Wright refers to community learning as "the learning that occurs when both the transactional mode and the client focus involve the community as a primary actor". Translated, this means that as adults perform community roles they are learning and also contributing to improving the community or at least raising their level of consciousness as it relates to community improvement. Wright implies that community learning is essential in the development of the individual and the community in a democratic society. Community learning and social learning are inextricably bound together. Learning in this sense reflects a verb instead of a noun. Thomas discusses several characteristics of social learning:

- Learning is action-oriented
- Individuals learn, not groups
- Learning is encouraged by others
- Learning is a reaction to stimuli
- Learning cannot be forced

There is a paucity of explicit learning theories of community development in the literature. There are numerous inferences regarding learning, which is usually discussed as a two-way process that occurs simultaneously with the other operational components of community development. An understanding of social and community learning further fortifies the proposition that learning is self-oriented, experientially driven, and social-role related.

SUMMARY

The concept of *community-based education*, which is synonymous with *nonformal education*, was defined and described. It is a form of education that is compatible with a bottom-up approach to community development where control and impetus lie in the hands of local people. Most of the recorded experience of nonformal education comes from campaigns and projects in non-industrial countries. Nonformal education is viewed not as a strategy to supplant formal education, but as a complementary process designed to address community problem solving from the perspective of local citizen participation.

A basic definition cf community development was discussed, with emphasis on the educational aspect. This particular emphasis is often marginalized or absent in the literature of community development. The traditional models have, for the most part, reflected top-down institutionalized approaches with very definite economic outcome goals. This was revealed through brief descriptions of community development in four countries: the United States, Britain, India, and Nigeria. The institutional control and economic outcome factors seem to be dominant in India and Nigeria.

The process and task orientations of community development were discussed in the context of short- and long-range goals of community development. The two dimensions are not mutually exclusive and can often be observed occurring together in a single development effort. However, primary emphasis is usually placed on either a process or a task orientation to community development. Nonformal education and community development are emerging fields of study and practice, multidisciplinary in cognitive content and application.

3

Community Control and Local Participation in Education

INTRODUCTION

Sometimes the term is used to identify a specific set of physical, cultural, and psychological characteristics of the members of a particular group who interact with each other based on common goals and issues (e.g., in the United States the "business community"). Basically, in community development work, community refers to a group of people who reside in the same geographical location. In this book *community* is geographically defined as an identifiable resident population base of people who share certain structural and functional relationships. These communities may be situated in urban, suburban, or rural areas.

The degree to which communities empower themselves is a reflection primarily of the quality and effectiveness of the horizontal relationships within the community as a whole. Sociological theories assume the critical importance of social networks in the community. A *primary* social network is one where sets of people help and support each other for personal reasons. A *secondary* social network consists of individuals in the community who associate with organized groups to pursue specific goals. Both social network levels are important to community empowerment. From the New Deal to the Great Society era in the United States, centralized government social programs have often failed to resolve problems at the community and neighbourhood levels. In most of these efforts, top-down approaches were the standard mode. Bottom-up approaches are needed that guarantee a large measure of community control by residents to initiate community-based adult education models relative to both the real and the felt needs of residents. All social networks must be recognized for the purpose of facilitating and enhancing increased local participation. In the past, some social scientists referred to some communities as "disorganized." This is a contradiction of the term. Community as a term and a concept implies organization. One prevailing stereotype about underdeveloped communities is that the residents are "apathetic." This is a dangerous stereotype because it is an easy way of "blaming the victim" without examining other complexities that would reveal a more realistic assessment of the community. What appears to be community apathy may be a reflection of other problems.

COMMUNITY APATHY

Community mobilization can be a long and tiring process in neighbourhoods where many citizens have not been involved in collective action. Many of these people resist ideas for social change and feel powerless about doing anything. Some do not see any problem or issue that arouse their interest, and others admit there is a problem, but do not believe that there is a solution. Many other residents in the neighbourhood offer the common excuse: "I'm too busy with other things!" All of these responses demonstrate the unwillingness of people to be involved. This conclusion points to a potential underlying theme of community apathy. There must be extreme caution in making this assumption because its consequences are counterproductive to building a neighbourhood organization for action. What appears to be apathy may be faulty methods in the mobilization process used by neighbourhood leadership. Foley suggests that six elements should be analyzed in assessing apathy in relation to leadership strategies:

1. **Planning.** The central question here is "Was it effective?" Lead time for planning is an important component because it allows leadership to identify the felt needs of residents and present those needs in a creative and forceful manner so as to ignite residents for collective action.
2. **Preparation.** Neighbourhood leaders are often poorly prepared to execute processes that have a direct relationship to the unique needs of the population. They often panic when met with resistance and indifference. Frequently conflicts arise and are not resolved through negotiations; thus, the neighbourhood is blamed for its apathy.
3. **Sponsorship.** Sometimes projects fail because the names of persons and groups associated with the sponsorship of the project evoke a negative reaction from the residents at large. Careful scrutiny of sponsorship by the leadership and their sensitivity to predictable group values improve the possibility of selecting acceptable sponsors.
4. **Timing.** Bad timing can cause a well-planned project or campaign to fail. Activities scheduled at the convenience of the leadership may often be inconvenient for residents. Leadership must be aware of competing activities and conditions on an annual basis so that scheduling can be effective.
5. **Leadership style.** Adult residents generally resist autocratic leaders. A plan or activity presented as the only solution, backed by unyielding leadership authority, is likely to fail. Effective leadership

strategies should stress openness and patience, with an emphasis on the democratic process.

6. **Approach.** The wrong approach to social action tends to elicit group opposition, rather than cooperation. Community action approaches must be customized to local attitudes, values, and conditions. A textbook approach may not work effectively with a particular population. Any approach should be flexible and easily modified as conditions dictate.

The foregoing six elements suggest that there are multiple factors to be analyzed before characterizing residents of a community. These elements provide a filter through which a neighbourhood leadership analysis can be ascertained. What frequently is labelled apathy is often caused by an operational flaw in one or more of the six elements. This suggests that the quality of leadership is critical to the success of collective action. Some generic concerns about the politics of local control need to be addressed at this juncture.

POLITICS OF LOCAL CONTROL

The idealism of a participatory democratic society can be achieved only through local control. As central governments grow and expand their control, the possibilities for meaningful political activity by the masses decline. The struggle for local control is a worldwide phenomenon. The object of community power requires that people question the control by constitutional charters and ruling oligarchies. They must make demands for cooperation and a greater sharing of resources, which are needed to develop their communities. This strategy has implications for industrial and nonindustrial countries. In North America the leverage of the ballot box can be used to demonstrate the collective strength of the community.

Traditionally, neighbourhoods were sometimes seen as independent political units that set their own customs and standards and made decisions about taxing, zoning, and other matters. As most countries in the world have experienced urbanization, the major complexion of neighbourhood control has been transformed. Today, neighbourhood residents are members of political units controlled by the power of a centralized authority, and thus subject to its political control. City council members and other professional politicians of the party in power make decisions on important matters affecting the quality of neighbourhood life. The pendulum for change has been swinging many years toward a resurgence of resident demands for local control. Demands for neighbourhood control of public social programs have been growing for the past twenty-five years in the United States. The ability to select and shape one's neighbourhood is a key part of any participatory democracy.

Glazer surmises that the issue of community control is part of a major trend against the increasing bureaucratization and centralization of local government. Warren state that "*The demand for community control can be seen, then, as a response to the political modernization of American cities. Community control of urban bureaucracies is offered as a means of making these bureaucracies more responsive to the needs of their clients*". Generally, central government is not organized to expedite the resolution of problems in a timely manner. In some cases what appears to be a decentralized form of neighbourhood government often exacerbates the problems because it creates another bureaucratic layer of government.

A specific example of this is the Advisory Neighbourhood Commission (ANC) system of Washington, D.C. Established by law in 1975, the system is designed to serve as a type of neighbourhood government. The city has 35 ANCs determined by census tract boundaries and each containing approximately 20,000 to 25,000 residents. Furthermore, each ANC is then divided into twelve single-member districts (SMDs), with about 2,000 people in each SMD. Each SMD elects a representative to serve on the ANC. Single-member Districts representatives must hold meetings with their residents at least four times a year to get their views on problems affecting the area. The D.C. City Council appropriates funds to all ANCs annually. The funding levels cover administrative costs but not programs or services for residents.

During the past ten years, reactions from D.C. residents have been mixed regarding the efficiency of the ANC model of neighbourhood government. Many residents, particularly in the African-American neighbourhoods, contend that most of the ANC representatives have been co-opted by the D.C. City Council for the purpose of minimizing organized protest and other demands of residents. In contrast, many residents voice support for progressive ANCs in the city who speak out and bring political and community pressure to bear on problems such as zoning, unfair business practices, housing speculation, rent control, public school issues, and taxes. Clearly, another layer of the bureaucracy has been created with the election of an additional 350 plus "quasi-politicians" who purport to represent community residents. Government reaction time is also lengthened because of the requirement for neighbourhood hearings.

The idea of local control is not new or unique because people have the natural capacity to develop appropriate action responses to solve many of their own problems. Central government has a vital role to play, in that it is most efficient when it has sufficient time to offer very specialized assistance and to mount large-scale programs and services. There are vested interests and political complexities that face communities as they demand their proportion of control. Collaborative strategies and linkages must be provided for a balanced approach, which is necessary to keep one from dominating the other. Warren pose this question: "With so many vested interests at stake, how is such a delicate balance achieved and maintained?".

NEIGHBOURHOOD ORGANIZATIONS

Community-based organizations are the local support systems that are initiated, controlled, and maintained by neighbourhood residents to accomplish various process- and task-oriented goals of community development. Some organizations are formed to tackle problems related to crime and drugs, others to promote economic development, and some to galvanize citizen support for a particular political issue. Some are formed to lobby for greater resources from public helping and support systems. Organizations that tend to be task-oriented, rather than process-oriented, have a shorter life-cycle and will usually abandon operations when the task is accomplished. However, there are literally thousands of neighbourhood organizations that have been in continuous existence for more than fifty years.

Mico discusses the organization and workings of community controlled organizations. There are three types that are prevalent in the United States: community-based organizations (CBOs), community action agencies (CAAs), and community development corporations (CDCs).

COMMUNITY-BASED ORGANIZATIONS (CBOs)

"A community-based organization is a formalized social structure that enables many people to work together in the pursuit of a common goal. It is controlled by the people in the neighbourhood or community". Generally, CBOs are not affiliated with national or state organizations, which would require them to operate under the constraints, bylaws, or control of another authority. They can receive grants or contracts from private or governmental sources and must abide by funding guidelines, but these do not control the organization. Formalization of CBOs varies; some may be incorporated, have a board of directors, have paid and volunteer staff, and conduct technical long- and short-range programs or they may be characterized by some combination of the foregoing. Due to government budget reductions in the United States, the current trend for CBOs is to seek funding from many sources. CBOs that have well-defined and focused goals tend to survive longer and stimulate greater citizen involvement for self-determination.

COMMUNITY ACTION AGENCIES (CAAs)

These are quasi-governmental organizations to the extent of the proportion of funding derived from federal and local government sources. Government agencies are in control of programs funded by them. CAAs were popularized in the 1960s as umbrella anti-poverty agencies in partnership with local government. The CAA of today is a general-purpose program designed to mobilize human and financial resources in order to attack poverty and other social ills at the source.

CAAs stress citizen involvement through a strategic planning process that assesses needs, develops resources, prioritizes goals, identifies approaches, and establishes evaluation procedures. Some of the typical programs mounted by CAAs are educational programs for adults, youth, and preschool children; community development, which encourages citizen participation; job training and placement; senior citizens' recreational programs and housing; health screening and social services; housing rehabilitation and restoration; and rural transportation.

COMMUNITY DEVELOPMENT CORPORATIONS (CDCs)

Initially funded by the Ford Foundation in the 1960s, CDCs served as experimental programs with a focus on economic development. The underlying rationale is that if the economic problems of the poor could be improved, this would help improve their educational achievement, health status, and job skills and meet their housing needs. CDCs are targeted to special impact area with high unemployment and low incomes. CDCs are funded from multiple government and private sources. About 10 percent receive funding from the U.S. Office of Economic Development under Title VII Special Impact Funds. Some CDCs are involved in setting up profit-making businesses, investing in corporations, and providing venture capital grants and loan guarantees. Each CDC is required to develop an overall economic development plan, which reflects the economic needs of the community served. The long-range single goal is to raise the economic level of the targeted community to be on par with the surrounding jurisdiction.

Community and neighbourhood organizations seek to organize residents around common issues. **Perlman** erroneously notes that "*the difference between those of fifty years ago and those of today is that the former struggled for social changes at the point of production, in the factories, through unions, whereas today, the struggle is at the point of consumption, with the users of services and the payers of taxes*". One may argue that this assumption is not entirely accurate as we examine the range of socio-economic levels that exist in communities worldwide. For thousands of community residents who today find themselves politically and economically disenfranchised, the struggle continues to focus on policy formulation and on representation in the decision-making process relative to issues that affect their daily lives.

LOCAL LEADERSHIP

The building of effective community-based organizations cannot be accomplished without local leadership. Every community has its own array of indigenous leaders. At the *formal* level they may be people serving in appointed and elected positions (e.g., local ministers, teachers, village chiefs, ward representatives, or former politicians). At the *informal* level they may come from the ranks of ordinary grass-roots citizens who happen to be charismatic and persuasive, possess natural leadership attributes, are streetwise, and are linked to a network of many potential followers in the community. The single thread that connects both of the groups is the capability to mobilize neighbors. They do this by arousing resident interest, influencing people to get involved, changing attitudes, and awakening their natural interest for self-determination. The formal and informal levels of neighbourhood leadership exist in all communities. Sometimes they intersect and cooperate in resolving community problems. Sometimes they maintain separate postures. In defining and describing neighbourhood leadership, sociologists in the past have used three basic approaches. First is to ask a cross-section of people in the neighbourhood this question: who are the individuals making important contributions to the community? Second is to identify persons in leadership roles in organizations within and outside the community. Third is to analyze specific issues faced by the community and identify persons who played important roles in the resolution of these issues. The first is similar to Hunter "power structure" community analysis, which identifies leaders in four elements: business, government, civic associations, and society activities. However, Hunter's most important finding was that "the patterns of leadership and power in the minority community and community-at-large are different. The power structure in the Black or Puerto Rican communities is not a mirror-like reflection of the white community's power structure". The studies of Warren revealed that there are three levels of neighbourhood leadership:

1. **Officers of local organizations.** This is the formal leadership role, consisting of people appointed or elected to an official leadership position. They also may be part of the informal network.
2. **Neighbourhood activities.** These are individuals who have established a track record for initiating action. Usually these persons are not members of an organization, but operate within the sphere of a network of followers. Many of these persons are found in the neighbourhood.
3. **Opinion leaders.** These persons command recognition that propels residents to seek them out for information, advice, or knowledge about a specific issue. Usually not members of a formal group, they

tend to be "loners" and prefer to share information instead of organizational involvement.

Since the informal network represents the majority of residents, special attention should be given to this leadership stratum. Classically, when neighbourhood leaders are approached by external agencies or identified in the news media, they are almost always persons from the formal leadership stratum. Typically, these "leaders" are chosen by sources extra-local to the neighbourhood. The real danger here is that they may not have the critical mass of neighbourhood support and following leaders representing both the formal and the informal levels have critical roles to play in the division of labor relative to social action.

The structure of neighbourhood leadership tends to reverse itself when viewed in black and white neighbourhoods in the United States. In the black community, women tend more to be the formal leaders, and men the informal leaders. The opposite tendency applies to the white community. The important overall need for neighbourhood unity is to link the formal and informal levels for optimal development and action. A diversity of leadership styles exists in all communities. The ultimate leadership goal is not one of developing leadership, but one of building a synergistic leadership climate, which will allow all leadership styles to flourish for the unification of community organization and effective action.

CITIZEN PARTICIPATION

Mobilizing people involves meeting them and explaining why they should be involved in a community organization. Basic to community development is the ability to mobilize people for involvement through participation. Generally, people who are informed about a community issue and are interested in resolving it feel that they can be more effective in working with a group. A nationwide survey in the United States found that 74 percent of those surveyed would rather associate with others to exact influence than act alone. One of the keys to citizen participation is convincing people that the community issue is one of common concern. Ross and Lappin discuss this aspect of participation as capitalizing on feelings of discontent with existing conditions, which fuels the need to organize, plan, and take action. Committed participation, at the group level, results when a sufficiently large group of people arrives at a consensus regarding the need for and the direction of social change. There are certain value assumptions that should be understood by neighbourhood leadership in efforts to promote citizen participation. **Cary** states them as follows: "(1) people of the community should actively participate in community change; (2) participation should be as inclusive as possible; and (3) participation should be through democratic organizations. Three necessary conditions for participation must be present if these value assumptions are to be realized: (1) freedom to participate autonomy; (2) ability to participate; and (3) willingness to participate".

Poverty was identified as a serious social problem in the United States during the 1960s. The Economic Opportunity Act of 1964 marked the first time in history that poor Americans were allowed to participate in the planning of anti-poverty programs. The law required "maximum feasible participation" of the poor in the planning process, but their inclusion did not come about as the law required. In some programs only token citizen participation was allowed. There is an old stereotype that "the poor do not have the ability to participate." For example, in the early Head Start programs, the planning was done by school board educators. In a few instances where poor parents were encouraged, they were not only effective in the program aspect of planning, but also able to relate these experiences to the problems of their neighbourhoods. These experiences gave poor parents exposure and skills that led to the organization of community councils and to concern for improved living conditions in the neighbourhoods. These earlier experiences of citizen participation by the poor have had a spillover effect on neighbourhood development in America on two levels. First, the stereotype that poor people are unable to plan was exploded. Second, as a result of skills gained by the poor, they have been able to transfer planning methodology for early childhood education to neighbourhood planning for improved living conditions.

Studies of political participation focus on which groups will be easy to mobilize and how to excite people who voice support for an organization but rarely get fully involved. As **Milbrath** indicates, "*About 8 percent of the population are involved in some community organization, about 14 percent contact government officials, 30 percent work with others on local problems, while only a handful, 3 percent, claim they would participate in public demonstrations*". Studies of federally sponsored community development organizations report that 13 to 14 percent of the population claim any kind of involvement.

Some studies indicate that participation in political and social organizations is higher among the highly educated and majority group members; the wealthy participate more than the poor; and white-collar workers participate more than blue-collar workers. Some of these findings are misleading regarding the participation of black Americans. Much of the research has focused on political issues at the national and regional levels or has related to the larger social fabric. Undereducated low-income blacks and other minorities have traditionally been passive participants in national politics, which deals with issues outside their realm of experience and immediate community-based needs. Minorities respond with enthusiastic levels of participation "to an arena of concrete, visible concerns such as their own block". People from higher economic classes feel directly affected by major political issues, so they participate more.

"But when people are interested in particular local problems, they will participate irrespective of class or race". At the community and neighbourhood levels, participation at higher levels is possible, given the assumption that neighbourhood leadership has the ability to illuminate issues and gain consensus on the severity of the issue for participation, planning, and action. Sustained participation is an objective of the overall goal of participation. It is very much contingent upon the recognition of important measures that determine the degree to which people are involved in the democratic process of decision making. Great care and sensitivity must be exercised for the inclusion of this ideal. An understanding of group needs as they relate to the decision-making process can facilitate and ensure a democratic system.

GROUP NEEDS AND DECISION MAKING

Leaders and facilitators of groups have the responsibility to display certain skills and attitudes in their attempts to create an atmosphere of openness and inclusiveness. It is essential to understand the basic needs of people in groups. The following is a listing of group needs:

- sense of belonging;
- share in planning;
- reasonable group goals;
- worthwhile group activities;
- input in making group rules;
- clear expectation of membership;
- challenging tasks;
- sense progress;
- information;
- confidence in the leader.

These ten simple needs are reflected by most people, regardless of socio-economic level or nature of the group. Obviously, some members of a group will have more difficulty in satisfying some of these needs than others. For example, a sense of belonging requires that people are made to feel welcome, that no one objects to their presence, and that they are made to feel needed. Whether this need is met is dependent on the behavior of the leader and also, to some extent, on the behavior of some of the members of the group. There are a series of *task* and *maintenance* functions that members of the group should display if the group is to engage in decision making that reflects consensus. Task functions refer to the content of the group's purpose. Task behaviors are directed to getting the job accomplished. Maintenance functions are dynamics that deal with morale, feelings, conflict, and cooperation. The goal of maintenance functions is to promote group harmony by creating an atmosphere where everyone can contribute. Every group, to achieve its goal, is constantly involved in making decisions: big decisions, little decisions; easy decisions, hard decisions; right decisions, wrong decisions but always decisions. Decision making is thus a continuing pattern of relationships among members of a group, a pattern over which every individual member has significant influence. It is amazing the effect that a bit of information here, a loud objection there, or an expression of approval or hostility, envy or admiration, contempt or condescension can have on an impending decision. So there is little wonder that group after group has difficulty making decisions. Some become paralyzed when confronted with a decision; some argue interminably over a minor point; others rush into a vote, only to reverse their decision later on or to fail in carrying it out; others appoint a committee or look for a savior (the chair) to save them from having to decide. Most of the difficulties encountered by a group in making decisions centre around one or another of the following factors:

- **Fear of consequence.** In some groups the possible outcome of an impending decision may bring divisions and disagreements. Frank acknowledgement of these fears often suggests how they can be dealt with effectively.
- **Conflicting loyalties.** Multiple membership in a number of groups frequently leads to divided loyalties

among group members. An atmosphere in which these conflicts can be brought out into the open without threat to the individual is a great help in their resolution.

- **Interpersonal conflict.** In groups of any size, personal differences occur that provoke feelings of affection or of antipathy among members and that inhibit sound decision making. Often another member who is not involved in the interpersonal conflict can bring the real problem into bolder relief.
- **Methodological blundering.** A group may be so bound by rigid procedures that there is little chance for free expression of differences. Or a group may allow itself to substitute personal opinion for adequate data. Or a group may approach the decision-making process without testing for consensus.
- **Inadequate leadership.** A facilitator falls short of the leadership responsibilities when the free expression of opinion is restricted and when there is a failure to provide assistance in selecting appropriate methods of decision making.

Effective decision making by a group on the basis of consensus is both realistic and possible. But it is not easy. There are five basic steps that a group can take in arriving at a decision with some assurance that it represents the mind of the group as a whole and that it will be acted upon. It is a good idea also to be aware of what may help a particular step, of what may block it, and of what may cause its omission.

1. **Defining the problem.** The process of defining the problem, sharpening the focus so that the issue is clear, internalizing its various implications, clarifying it, and elaborating on it.
2. **Suggesting alternative solutions.** The process of getting ideas on the various alternative solutions to the problem from all members.

3. **Testing the alternatives.** The process of examining the alternatives in the light of all available data, previous experience, possible consequences, relevance to the problem, and members' attitudes.
4. **Choosing among alternatives.** The process of reaching a decision by choosing one of the alternatives, or a combination of alternatives, that will provide a solution to the problem defined.
5. **Planning for action.** The process of making detailed plans for carrying out the decision by examining the implications of the choice and by testing the relevance of proposed action. It should be noted that the planning step sometimes results in rethinking the decision and returning to one or another prior step in the decision-making process.

SUMMARY

The initial task was to explore the notion of community apathy and its attendant negative consequences, which obscure the importance of politics regarding the ideal of community control. The politics of local control in relation to trends of government centralization as it impacts participatory democracy were discussed and briefly analyzed. The efforts to acquire degrees of community control were viewed as a universal ideal. This is particularly relevant to issues involving citizens' control of community development.

Several types of community-based organizations, which are found in the United States, were discussed from the perspective of their organizing goals. The community-based organization was viewed as the major vehicle that has to be assembled before any meaningful development can be initiated. A concomitant concern was the utilization of local leadership at the formal and informal levels as the human mechanism that energizes the community-based organization. A description of several types of local leaders found in most communities was presented in the context of citizen mobilization.

The crucial element of citizen participation is incorporated as an organization and leadership goal that is central to community development. The identification of issues is key to the mobilization of people. A major assumption is that, regardless of the socio-economic strata found in a community, citizens will come together if they perceive the issue(s) to be significant. A mass-base appeal is desirable, but community-based organizations need only to attract a critical mass of citizens for effective development efforts.

❑❑❑

4

Globalization of Adult Education and Training

INTRODUCTION

The key theme that can be seen to underlie the discussion throughout the chapter, therefore, is that of globalization, a process which has been affecting adult education and training at least as much as other fields. Globalization has been defined as:

> *the processes through which sovereign national states are crisscrossed and undermined by transnational actors with varying prospects of power, orientations, identities and networks.*

An historical process which engenders a shift in the spatial reach of networks and systems of social relations to transcontinental (or interregional) patterns of human organization, activity and the exercise of social power.

Globalization as an idea is much discussed at the present time. Two related aspects of this debate concern the extent to which globalization is actually happening, and whether it is being accompanied by a parallel localization and/or exclusion of sections of society. These debates can be traced throughout the examination of the concepts in this chapter. The concepts of lifelong education and the learning society first became the subject of extensive discussion during the 1960s and 1970s, though they have earlier antecedents. There were at least three main reasons for their articulation at that time:

- the (perception of the) increasing pace of economic, social and technological change on a global scale;
- the belief that existing education and training practices and provision were inadequate to cope; and
- the conviction that educational opportunities should be available to all.

These concepts were developed against a backcloth of critical debate regarding the role of formal institutions and curricula, led by influential writers such as Freire and Illich.

With the hindsight that thirty or forty years provides, some of these discussions may now seem to lack practical purchase and to convey undue optimism about the possibility for democratic change based on reasoned argument and widespread participation in education and training. The associated structures of the welfare state, interventionist government and supranational organization have all come in for a good deal of criticism in the last three decades. Yet the concepts of lifelong learning and the learning society have not gone away; on the contrary, as the discussion which follows demonstrates, in the last few years they have been reborn and become the subject of increasing attention at the level of both policy and research.

The concept of the learning organization is rather more recent in origin. It came to prominence in the 1980s, offering a meso, organizational level of analysis between the macro, societal focus evident in the concept of the learning society and the more micro, individual level of lifelong education.

LIFELONG EDUCATION

The concept of LLL [lifelong learning] emerged almost simultaneously in the Council of Europe, UNESCO and OECD in the late 1960s as 'recurrent education', 'adult education' or *éducation permanente*. The central idea was the same: the development of coherent strategies to provide education and training opportunities for all individuals during their entire life.

The origins of the concept have been traced back to the writings of Dewey, Lindeman and Yeaxlee in the early twentieth century. In essence, lifelong education and/or lifelong learning, like the other concepts discussed in this chapter, argue for a rejection of a model of education that is confined to childhood, adolescence and early adulthood. Instead, learning is portrayed as being available throughout life, as needed and desired, for everyone.

However, having attracted a great deal of interest, particularly at international level, in the 1960s and 1970s, discussion and usage of the concept then suffered a slump, only to return with a vengeance in the mid-1990s, this time at both international and national levels:

The European Union designated 1996 'the year of lifelong learning'. The meeting of the education ministers of the Organization for Economic Cooperation and Development in January of the same year used the slogan '*Making lifelong learning a reality for all*'. The 1996 report of the United Nations Educational, Scientific and Cultural Organization's International Commission on Education for the Twenty-first Century adopted 'learning throughout life' as its key concept. At their meeting in Cologne in June 1999 the members of the Group of Eight...agreed to promote mass education throughout the world, and named 'lifelong retraining' as a priority.

It seems reasonable, then, to ask why there has been this remarkable resurgence of interest in the concept. The most plausible explanation seems to be that, while the understanding of the concept and the content of the policy may vary, lifelong learning offers a useful label for policy-makers:

As a phrase, lifelong learning has in several European nations-generally with Social Democratic parties in power-become a convenient political shorthand for the modernizing of education and training systems. As in the intergovernmental agencies, it is often associated with attempts to increase competitiveness and innovation at a time of intensifying global trading pressures, by promoting investment in human resources across the life span and in a variety of settings. To this extent, it is becoming part of the accepted policy discourse of the western nations.

The implications of lifelong education have been usefully summarized by two of its main proponents in the following fashion:

> *Lifelong education is a set of organizational and procedural guidelines for educational practice. Its goal is lifelong learning-learning carried out throughout life. It is important to make clear at once that what is meant here by 'learning' is not the spontaneous, day-to-day learning of everyday life. The kind of lifelong learning that is the object of lifelong education has the following four definitive characteristics:*
>
> 1. *It is intentional-learners are aware that they are learning.*
> 2. *It has specific goals, and is not aimed at vague generalizations such as 'developing the mind'.*
> 3. *These goals are the reason why the learning is undertaken (i.e. it is not motivated simply by factors like boredom).*
> 4. *The learner intends to retain and use what has been learnt for a considerable period of time.*

While this summation may seem restrictive in its view of what counts as learning, three further features of the concept may be unpacked from this quotation and similar accounts. First, lifelong education is seen as building upon and affecting all existing educational providers, including both schools and institutions of higher education. Second, it extends beyond the formal educational providers to encompass all agencies, groups and individuals involved in any kind of learning activity.

There is, however, no 'standard' model of what a lifelong education system might look like. It is rather a slippery concept, which may be attractive to both totalitarian and liberal regimes, to both technologically developed and less developed societies and applied to both vocational and non-vocational curricula.

For instance, it is an instrument *for* change (in individuals, organizations and society) and as a buffer *against* change; it is a means of increasing economic competitiveness and of personal development; it is a social policy to combat social exclusion and to ease the re-entry of the unemployed into the labour market; it is a way of promoting the professional and social development of employees and of acquiring new knowledge through the labour process; and it is a strategy to develop the participation of citizens in social, cultural and political affairs. But there is also a sceptical version of lifelong learning which has received little attention namely that it has become a form of social control.

There are other theoretical objections to the idea of lifelong education, in addition to its lack of precision. Some writers have noted the way in which its proponents tend to equate education with learning, making little distinction between different forms or levels. Others have argued that the concept adds little to the notion of adult education. The practical objections are just as telling. At the system level, financial and structural concerns appear paramount. It is, of course, a characteristic of conceptual development that little attention is typically given to pragmatic concerns like costs, but this ignorance in most writing about lifelong education does appear significant: 'Without real teachers, given real resources to empower students, lifelong learning will remain a slogan, a catchphrase, a substitute for real action'. The sheer scale and vagueness of the concept also translates into policy. Thus: 'the last two decades have witnessed a flood of three lettered, alphabet soup initiatives connected with lifelong learning: for example: APL, CPD, EHE, EDPs, IiP, NVQs, OCNs and TECs'.

Some of these ingredients have since been relabelled or replaced. At the time of writing, the two most notable new ingredients to this soup were the University for Industry (UfI frequently criticized for not being a university in the commonly understood sense of the term) and Individual Learning Accounts (ILAs now discontinued because of fraud). A glance at the, regularly updated, lifelong learning website provided by the British Department for Education and Skills (www.lifelonglearning.co.uk) confirms the bewildering and changing variety of policies and projects, of all scales, which may be marshalled together to make up a government's lifelong learning strategy.

In a review of British government policy in this area, I aired three main concerns:

> *First, both in the policy documents themselves and in the translation from policy to practice, there seems to be a tendency to elide the broad view of lifelong learning for all with a narrower perspective on vocational education and training.second in listing a whole series of groups who tend not to participate in post-compulsory learning, the reports reviewed have usually identified their target groups for developing a learning society. The problem is, however, that this is typically done in a way which effectively blames non-participants and places upon them the responsibility for doing something about it. My third concern is with the apparently compulsory aspect of the lifelong learning policies being articulated.*

The emphasis that these policies place on individuals, for taking responsibility (and paying) for their lifelong learning, is perhaps their most fundamental flaw. This may work for the well educated and the professional, who have been successful in the educational system and can perceive additional advantages from continued participation. It is hardly likely to work, however, for those who left formal education early, with little or nothing in the way of qualifications, but with bad memories and resentments, and who have been, relatively speaking, socially and economically excluded ever since.

LEARNING ORGANIZATION

The idea of the learning organization arises, like those of lifelong education and learning, from global concerns about change and survival. While the articulation of the concept took place as late as the 1980s, at least three interrelated precursors for it (or pressures leading to it) may be identified.

The first of these derives from the concern of management consultants with how to encourage organizational as distinct from individual or group learning. Organizational learning is seen as something greater than the sum of the elements of individual and group learning of which it is comprised. It represents, therefore, an interaction between the organization's component parts and the outside environment to the benefit of the organization as a whole. This school of thought is associated in particular with Argyris and Schön, and their work on organizational development, professionalism, theories of action and reflective practice. Their writing on organizational learning is grounded within systems thinking:

> *Organizational learning involves the detection and correction of error. When the error detected and corrected permits the organization to carry on its present policies or achieve its present objectives, then that error-detection-and-correction process is* single-loop *learning...* Double-loop *learning occurs when error is detected and corrected in ways that involve the modification of an organization's underlying norms, policies and objectives.*

The second line of thinking behind the learning organization has to do with the competitive necessities imposed by global economic and technological changes, the drive towards permanent and sustained innovation, and consequent concerns with quality and value for money. These issues are reflected in the writings of management gurus like Drucker, Lessem, Peters and Senge. This line of thinking has found expression in the ideas of total quality management and its derivative, total quality learning. It underlies a number of recent initiatives, such as the Management Charter and Investors in People.

The third precursor for the current concern with the learning organization may be traced in changing industrial relations practice. Increasing numbers of companies operating in the less regulated industrialized economies, such as the United States and the United Kingdom, have sought to provide general educational and developmental opportunities for their employees. They typically offer an annual sum for each employee to spend on some kind of learning activity, in addition to enhanced in-company training and development opportunities. We may speculate upon the differing motivations of the managers and union representatives involved in agreeing such non-wage rewards: perhaps staff retention and motivation in the former case, and membership retention or expansion in the latter. But such employee development initiatives have caught the imagination, and are now frequently seen as a key component of the learning organization.

As may be judged from the discussion so far, the idea of the learning organization applies many of the same ideas as lifelong education and the learning society, but at the organizational or company, rather than the individual or societal level:

> *The Learning Company is a vision of what might be possible. It is not brought about simply by training individuals; it can only happen as a result of* learning at the whole organisation *level. A Learning Company is an organization that facilitates the learning of all its members* and *continuously transforms itself.*

That reads as a rather top-down, managerially imposed view, and raises the questions of who participates in, and who has authority over, such learning. Much the same sentiments have been expressed, however, in what may be seen as a more democratic, bottom-up fashion:

> *Learning organizations are characterized by total employee involvement in a process of collaboratively initiated, collaboratively conducted, collectively accountable change directed towards shared values or principles.*

A third definition appears to offer elements of both of these approaches:

> *A learning organization is one that has a climate that accelerates individual and group learning. Learning organizations teach their employees the critical thinking process for understanding what it does and why it does it. These individuals help the organization itself to learn from mistakes as well as successes. As a result, they recognize changes in their environment and adapt effectively. Learning organizations can be seen as a group of empowered employees who generate new knowledge, products and services; network in an innovative community inside and outside the organization; and work towards a higher purpose of service and enlightenment to the larger world.*

While that last phrase sounds just a little too altruistic, these authors, linking the idea of the learning organization to globalization, go on to identify a model for the global learning organization. They list eleven essential organizational elements for global learning: appropriate structures, a corporate learning culture, empowerment, environmental scanning, knowledge creation and transfer, quality, strategy, supportive atmosphere, teamwork and networking and vision. Despite the high demands thus placed on becoming and remaining a learning organization, many organizations have been held up as examples, or at least as aspirants. These have included, in the United Kingdom, Nabisco, Rover, Sheerness Steel and Sun Alliance and further afield, General Electric, Honda, Samsung and Xerox.

A range of 'how to' publications exist which aim to demonstrate to managers and others how they can change their organizations into learning organizations. These are relatively clear in identifying the prospective benefits to the main 'stakeholders' involved: the organization's customers, employees and shareholders. For example:

> *Benefits for customers include making available to customers products and services that meet their evolving requirements more effectively than competitors the rate of innovation, not just in products and services, but in process adaptability and responsiveness. Benefits for employees*

> *include the ability to enhance both internal and external employability the opportunity for better job security a sense of self-respect. Benefits for shareholders include differentiated human assets that have more value than those of the competition minimising voluntary losses of good people the reduction in layers of management the reduction of costs as continuous improvement yields continuous productivity increase the elimination of duplication and overlapping activity the ability to seize market opportunities through speed of adaptation and change the availability of the right people with the right skills in the right place at the right time.*

Given such an impressive list, one might wonder why all organizations are not seeking to become learning organizations as quickly as possible. Could it be that the idea is as diaphanous and unrealizable as the ideals of lifelong learning and the learning society? Or might it be that the learning organization is just one in a long line of management buzzwords, which come off the guru conveyor belt and on to the airport bookstalls most weeks? Or perhaps it is only applicable to and by certain sorts of organizations?

While interesting as a theoretical construct the idea of the LO may be of limited value in serving as a blueprint for skills policies in the majority of UK organizations. In particular, its lack of contact with the often harsh realities of cost and time pressures and external environmental constraints raises serious problems it seems reasonable to argue that there is little chance of achieving any very high level of organizational learning in the following circumstances, all of which are too prominent in the UK: cost-based competition; standardized products and services; a heavy reliance on economy-of-scale advantages; low-trust relationships; hierarchical management structures; people management systems that emphasize command, control and surveillance; an underlying belief that (whatever the overt rhetoric) people are a cost or a disposable factor of production; little slack or space for creativity; and a culture of blame where mistakes (particularly those of lower-status workers) are punished.

Other criticisms that may be levelled at the idea of the learning organization are many and varied. Thus, amongst those organizations that call themselves, or have been called, learning organizations, there are substantial variations in practice and experience. This can readily be demonstrated by, for example, the differences in who is included within the ambit of the learning organization: full-time staff, permanent staff, part-timers, all grades, customers, all plants, subsidiaries? It has also been questioned whether the learning organization is about empowerment or exploitation. Is it in the business of creatively seeking the views and inputs of all its members, and giving them due credit and say in their use; or is it about squeezing as much value as possible out of each unit of production, with the resulting profits channelled in traditional ways? Any concept that can encompass such radically differing viewpoints has major problems as well as considerable potential.

Then there is the issue-the 'bottom line' in management speak-of whether learning organizations actually do any better at their business than comparable 'non-learning' organizations. Here the evidence, as with that on general linkages between educational participation and economic productivity, is both partial and difficult to interpret. In other words, the consensual nature of idealizations such as the learning organization, which can become seen as the solution to problems of organizational survival and competitiveness, can act in counter-productive ways by denying the possibility of other solutions or progressions. In the final assessment:

> *A close look at the learning organization literature, with its rhetoric of trust and pledges of 'win-win', when contrasted with actions actually taken by many organizations defines a significant discontinuity between what is espoused and what really happens. Efforts expended in learning, in being flexible, in taking on additional responsibility and self-management go unrewarded in a contemporary capitalist economy.*

Most recently, the concept of the learning organization has come to be bracketed with, and to some extent supplanted by, that of knowledge management. The key difference in the latter is the added emphasis placed on the role of developing information technology, as the following analysis indicates:

> *Why did knowledge come to the top of the management agenda in the 1990s? Our analysis suggests that a number of factors have come together at this time. These fall under six headings:*
>
> - *wealth being demonstrably and increasingly generated from knowledge and intangible assets;*
> - *the rediscovery that people are the locus of much organizational knowledge;*
> - *accelerating change in markets, competition and technology, making continuous learning essential;*
> - *the recognition that innovation is the key to competitiveness, and depends on knowledge creation and application;*
> - *the growing importance of cross-boundary knowledge transactions;*
> - *technology limits and potential: the limits of information systems and the potential of communications and knowledge technologies.*

Aside from and despite this difference in emphasis, the criticisms which may be levelled at the concept of knowledge management remain much the same as those made of the learning organization:

> *Much about knowledge's recent rise to prominence has the appearance of faddishness and evangelism. Look in much of the management literature of the late 1990s and you could easily believe that faltering business plans need only embrace knowledge to be saved. While it's often hard to tell what this embracing involves, buying more information technology seems a key indulgence.*

LEARNING SOCIETY

While the learning society has only recently become the subject of considerable debate in the United Kingdom, it has a longer history in other countries that have a post-war tradition of greater educational participation. These include, for example, Canada, New Zealand, Sweden and the United States of America. In those societies the advent of discussion on the learning society may be linked not just to lifelong and recurrent education, but also to the development of ideas like the post-industrial society and the information society. In the United Kingdom, by contrast, the contemporary connections are as much with the issues of active citizenship and the learning polity.

Two recent, somewhat contrasting, British definitions of the learning society are:

> *A learning society would be one in which all citizens acquire a high quality general education, appropriate vocational training and a job (or series of jobs) worthy of a human being while continuing to participate in education and training throughout their lives. A learning society would combine excellence with equity and would equip all its citizens with the knowledge, understanding and skills to ensure national economic prosperity and much more besides. Citizens of a learning society would, by means of their continuing education and training, be able to engage in critical dialogue and action to improve the quality of life for the whole community and to ensure social integration as well as economic success.*

A learning society is much more than a society whose members are simply well educated. It is a place or a society where the idea of learning infuses every tissue of its being: a place where individuals and organizations are encouraged to learn about the dynamics of where they live and how it is changing; a place that on that basis changes the way it learns whether through schools or any other institution that can help foster understanding and learning; a place in which all its members are encouraged to learn; finally and perhaps most importantly a place that can learn to change the conditions of its learning democratically.

These definitions suggest both the conflictual and potentially all encompassing nature of the learning society. Thus, it may be seen as spanning both vocational concerns (the link between education and economy) and quality of life issues (the link between education and personal and social development). Some, of course, define the learning society rather more narrowly, focusing on just one of these poles of interest. As defined here, however, the concept clearly builds upon the notions of lifelong learning and the learning organization, and makes use of the underlying ideas of productivity and change.

The tensions apparent within existing discussions on the learning society have been a topic of considerable debate:

> *'The learning society' is an ambiguous term. It is descriptive, pointing to complexities and underlining the centrality of change; it is analytical, suggesting the possibility that modern society may be continuing to learn about itself and steering itself along its chosen path; it is normative, urging the need for learning to have a high profile at both the individual and the societal level; and it is ontological, making a statement about the fundamental nature of modern society and pointing to the centrality of rationality. On each interpretation education emerges as the key institution in modern society, but education conceived in terms broader than curricula framed by the academic community for young people.*

Other authors have focused on identifying the alternative interpretations that have been placed on the concept, for example:

1. The learning society as an *educated society,* committed to active citizenship, liberal democracy and equal opportunities.
2. The learning society as a *learning market,* enabling institutions to provide services for individuals as a condition for supporting the competitiveness of the economy.
3. The learning society as *learning networks,* in which learners adopt a learning approach to life, drawing on a wide range of resources to enable them to develop their interests and identities.

Three interpretations of the learning society: as an idealised conception of society–a futuristic ideal; as a reaction to social change–a reflexive society; and as a market phenomenon of the information socicty–a consumer society.

While Edwards's first and third interpretations, and Jarvis's first and second, have clear resonances with the ideals of lifelong education, it is the second interpretation, Edwards argues (and Jarvis's third), which is currently dominant. This reflects the emphasis of present policy on the perceived need, in an increasingly competitive global economy, for the effective development and availability of all human resources. Yet, at least in the definitions quoted earlier, the concern for the growth of the individual and the community still remains.

While broader visions of the learning society can be seen as an improvement on strict vocationalism, they do represent something of an unhappy and unstable compromise. As a banner under which a diversity of interests politicians, educators, industrialists can gather, the learning society embodies an alliance between state, professions and capital. Such an alliance seems likely to marginalize the interests of the individual in pursuing learning for their own self-fulfilment. Yet, at the same time, learning society policies seem to place undue reliance on individuals:

> *The main thrust of policy in both the UK and the EC is to give the pivotal role in constructing the Learning Society to the individual. The creation of a new form of society cannot be placed solely on the shoulders of individuals. It is a responsibility which must be shared by all the social partners government, employers, trade unions, voluntary organizations and individuals.*

Most of the criticisms that have been levelled at both lifelong education and the learning organization can also be levelled at the learning society. To their credit, the ESRC, quoted above, went on to question the notion of the learning society:

> *Some of the claims made on behalf of the learning society need to be subjected to empirical test; for example, does learning pay? does it empower and enable? does it help to equalise life chances? Will the purposes of education and training for the learning society need to encompass more than selection, socialisation, and minimal levels of literacy and numeracy in preparation for the world of work? What changes in education and training will be needed for all to participate fully in the learning society? Is there a set of values or guiding principles underpinning the notion of a learning society which need to be made explicit if a culture of education and training is to be created in the UK? What would a coherent and coordinated policy to help the UK become a learning society look like?*

Other commentators have also pointed out the considerable disparity between the rhetoric and present reality. Though survey evidence is conflicting in the United Kingdom, it is clear that adult participation rates-whether in formal education and training or in learning more broadly conceived do not match the rhetoric associated with the concept of the learning society. While a rather larger claim might be made for some other countries, even in these cases it is at best a partial vision of the learning society that is being achieved, with many still excluded. And when consideration is given to the embedded nature of the structural inequalities associated with access to education and training in all countries, we are left with a sense of disillusionment that a learning society in its fullest sense will ever be achieved.

IDEALS AND FASHIONS

A number of conclusions may be drawn from the analysis in this chapter. Three of these will be briefly discussed here.

First, we may question just how different the concepts are in their meanings and applications. Even a brief engagement with some of the sources quoted in this chapter will show the reader how common it is to find the concepts linked together, or even defined in terms of each other. Thus, discussions of lifelong education or learning typically also refer to the learning society, and vice-versa. And, while debates about the learning organization may take us into a different literature, that dealing with business and management, the links between this concept and the other two are also clear.

Second, the realism of these concepts as models for national or organizational systems of provision has to be questioned. We have already argued that none of them have been achieved in practice at any level, but we might also consider whether they are, by their very nature, achievable or not. It has been argued that these concepts are both

Utopian in nature and have the characteristics of myths. This was recognized at the time of their development by at least some of their proponents:

> *Reference to the concept met with many reservations, if not hostile attitudes. Some educators expressed the view that lifelong education was nothing more than a new term to designate adult education and that its use led to confusion. Others, while recognizing the rationality underlying the concept, looked upon it as Utopian, reaching far beyond the possibilities of implementation of a great number of countries.*

Ideals are, of course, widely used to inform and drive policy development. But, if they remain well beyond the possibility of achievement, their effectiveness may be limited.

Third, the history of these concepts appears to tell us something about changing fashions in adult education and training, as well as, on a larger scale, in political ideology. Lifelong education and the learning society have come into and out of fashion, and now are most definitely back in fashion again, although the meanings attached to the terms may have subtly changed. The learning organization, for its part, appears to have peaked in popularity and may now be being replaced by the idea of knowledge management. Clearly, we need such labels, but their changing meaning and usage is of critical importance.

Globalization refers primarily to changes occurring in the world economy as trade barriers are reduced, as capital becomes more mobile, and as multinational companies become larger and more powerful. The world economy is changing qualitatively from an international economy based on relationships between discrete national economies and toward a global economy in which multinational, global capital dominates nation-states. Civil societies, historically, have been supported by adult education, which equips adults with the skills and knowledge to participate in public life; and adults become educated through civic participation cultural, political, social. If adult education comes to mean only workplace training, it no longer will be able to support non-market civic and societal goals. The networks of NGOs and community groups focused on global concerns about the environment, human rights, women's rights, and indigenous cultures, as evidence that globalization is also proceeding "from below", a process that will could lead to a "global civil society."

Childhood schooling is in the background of these articles as adults are described as not having had access to quality childhood schooling.

Colleges for example, become sites for branding and the targets of corporate expansion. Many policymakers automatically look to market 'solutions'. The impact and pervasiveness of these forces of globalization also means that they should be a fundamental focus for education and learning but there are powerful currents running against honest work in this area. In this article we will explore some of what we believe to be the more significant aspects with regard to the practice and experience of education. These include:

- Commodification and the corporate takeover of education.
- The threat to the autonomy of national educational systems by globalization.
- De-localization and changing technologies and orientations in education.
- Branding, globalization and learning to be consumers.

This is not an exhaustive listing of issues but it does bring out some of the key dynamics and highlights some important areas of action and reaction for educators and learners with respect to globalization.

❑❑❑

noncampus environments industry, trade unions, the military, proprietary vocational schools, among others.

The distinction made here is based not on age, but on the nature and institutional location of the studies undertaken. There is also an implicit suggestion of a difference in terms of level (and perhaps status) and extent of commitment. Thus, higher education may be seen as operating at a 'higher' level, demanding a lengthier period of study, and involving more abstract and theoretical learning. This distinction also embodies elements of the vocational/liberal split discussed elsewhere, with further education portrayed as the more explicitly vocational form of provision.

Yet, in institutional terms, as already suggested, the distinction in provision and roles is not that clear cut. Some universities and colleges offer, as part of their overall provision, forms of education and training that fit the Carnegie definition of further education. Similarly, some institutions other than those identified offer academic degree programmes, including, increasingly, some industrial and commercial companies.

In England and Wales (Scotland has a somewhat different system of educational provision), on the other hand, further and higher education have a rather different, though at root similar, meaning. Here, further education was initially defined by the 1944 Education Act, and subsequently modified and re-phrased by the 1988 Education Reform Act as:

> *(a) full and part-time education and training for persons over compulsory school age (including vocational, social, physical and recreational training); and (b) organised leisure-time occupation provided in connection with the provision of such education.*

This definition is clearly age-related, though persons over the compulsory school age might study elsewhere than in further education institutions. There is no specific mention of the level of study, so further education could be seen as encompassing higher education. In practice, however, further education and higher education institutions have long been treated (and funded) separately and differently by the British government. Interestingly, the definition makes greater reference to liberal (social, physical, recreational, leisure-time) than to vocational forms of provision.

The Further and Higher Education Act 1992, however, removed further education colleges from local government control, giving them independent corporate status:

> *The colleges were effectively turned into businesses run by a Chief Executive answerable to a board of governors. What they did was now to be determined by the marketplace. Public money which had been channelled through the local authorities was passed to the FEFC [Further Education Funding Council] which created a market of its own in 'funding units'. In addition, the colleges were to compete for income from TECs [Training and Enterprise Councils, which, together with the FEFC, have since been replaced by Learning and Skills Councils (LSCs)] (which were roughly the employers' equivalent of local authorities), from the local authorities themselves for adult and community education, from contracts and grants for specific purposes, and through the generation of fee income of various kinds.*

They have since become the flagship institutions for delivering the government's lifelong learning policies.

Higher education (and even the more specific, and more popular, term 'university') lacks a generally accepted, legalistic definition. Nevertheless, most British discussions treat this term as if it were fairly unproblematic. Hence, many available definitions appear to be superficially straightforward; for example:

> *In the United Kingdom, 'higher education' is taken generally to refer to advanced courses provided mainly though not exclusively by the universities, polytechnics [now also designated as universities], colleges or institutes of higher education. 'Advanced' in this context usually means beyond A-level standard, and in fact entrance requirements are typically stated in terms of A levels.*

As in the case of the American interpretation, here the term is linked to particular institutional forms, indeed much the same ones as selected in the United States. These definitions are, however, rather circular in nature. Higher education is that which is provided mainly by universities and similar institutions: while universities offer, either wholly or chiefly, higher education. There is nothing in either the American or British definitions quoted here which tells us what it is about higher education which makes it 'higher'; or how it differs from 'lower' or 'notso-high' education, other than simply by following on from it.

A few authors have, however, attempted to examine the meaning of the term in more depth; for example, in terms of what higher education does:

> *Higher education benefits its students and the community as a whole. For both it develops what psychologists call affect: attitudes, emotions, motivation, values and interpersonal skills based upon feelings for others. It develops cognition: knowledge, perception and thought. And it develops adaptable occupational skills by the application of cognition and affect:*

One author in particular has devoted a great deal of attention during the last decade to the changing contemporary nature and meaning of higher education:

> *'higher education' is essentially a matter of the development of the mind of the individual student. It is not just any kind of development that the idea points to. An educational process can be termed higher education when the student is carried on to levels of reasoning which make possible critical reflection on his or her experiences, whether consisting of propositional knowledge or of knowledge through action. These levels of reasoning and reflection are 'higher', because they enable the student to take a view (from above, as it were) of what has been learned. Simply, 'higher education' resides in the higher-order states of mind.*

This kind of reasoning takes us further and in a different direction, breaking away from the institutional or qualification-based focus of the definitions already quoted. It also provides some guidance as to how higher education might be identified at the individual and institutional levels. Barnett goes on to equate higher education with critical thinking and the critical life:

> *a higher education for a genuinely learning society-a higher education for the critical life-imposes three conditions. First, students have to be exposed to multiple discourses. Secondly, and more controversially, the student will be exposed to wider understandings, questionings and potential impacts of her [sic] intellectual field. What is further required is a committed orientation on the part of the student to this form of life.*

Such definitions are, in principle, applicable to all countries and systems; though this would, of course, rest upon a shared appreciation of what expressions like critical reflection, higher-order states, multiple discourses and a committed orientation mean.

ADULT AND CONTINUING

Both Adult education and Continuing education have contested-broader or narrower, traditional or modern, radical or conservative-meanings. While the latter concept is not in such wide use, and may have passed out of fashion where it is used, the former has worldwide acceptance. Here the focus is on what is meant, particularly in an institutional sense, by adult education or adult training.

In its more 'traditional' meaning, adult education refers not just to the age and status of its clients, but also encompasses the notion of participatory learning for its own sake and not for credit. As such, adult education is as much a movement as a set of institutions. It is often closely linked with the idea of liberal education, as in the term liberal adult education. This interpretation of adult education has also been termed the 'great tradition', the five distinguishing characteristics of which have been identified as being:

- It is committed to a particular curriculum, to the humane or liberal studies.
- Within this curriculum particular concern is shown for the social studies its interest is in learning as a means of understanding the great issues of life.
- It demands from students a particular attitude-the non-vocational attitude and therefore examinations and awards are deplored.

- It combines democratic notions about equality of educational opportunity with assumptions about the educability of normal adults.
- It has found in small tutorial groups meeting for guided discussion over a fairly long period its most effective educational technique.

Even at the time this account was written, however, the great tradition was recognised as being in decline, and was looked back upon, with regret, as a largely pre-Second World War phenomenon. More recently, with changes in public policy and funding, the retreat away from the liberal conceptions of the great tradition has become more of a rout. Some reflections may still be seen, however, in contemporary 'radical' forms of adult education, as well as in some kinds of community education.

In its widest sense, the concept of adult education may be taken to refer to all education for adults. As such, it occupies, like further and higher education combined, the whole territory of post-compulsory provision, and may even be seen to extend beyond this to include less institutionalized forms of provision as well. For many practitioners, however, especially those from an older generation, the distinction between 'adult education', narrowly defined, and the broader context of 'education for adults' continues to have significance:

> *The 'education of adults' can be seen to cover all forms of education (planned learning opportunities) for those over the age of 16 (or whatever), whether the student participants are treated as adults or as if they were younger learners-taught, that is, as if they were largely or completely ignorant of the subject being studied, without relevant experience, unable to be relied upon to control their own learning, having little or nothing to contribute to the learning process. 'Adult education', by contrast, consists of all those forms of education that treat the student participants as adults-capable, experienced, responsible, mature and balanced people.*

Many would reject both the straightforward distinctions between adults and children suggested here and the implied focus of attention on just one part of the broad field of adult education and training. Yet the concept of adult education still carries a wealth of meanings and perceptual baggage, in the United Kingdom and elsewhere, which may be seen to effectively limit its conceptual and practical usefulness:

> *The term 'adult education' carries specific connotations in the United Kingdom which imply that it is specifically liberal education, and this also has a stereotype of being a middle-class, leisure time pursuit. Underlying this implication is the idea that the adult's education has been completed and, during leisure time, the adult self-indulgently improves or broadens existing knowledge, skills or hobbies...it is hardly surprising that adult education is regarded as marginal.*

This quotation makes clear a very common view of adult education as an essentially spare-time activity. This activity is engaged in for interest or amusement by individuals whose major role is not that of a learner, but that of a worker, whether paid or unpaid, to which role education makes little contribution. The marginality of adult education, though seemingly welcomed by older practitioners, remains a problem today:

> *Since World War II the education of adults has neither been willing nor able to ignore its isolation from conventional education, that is, schooling. But it has accepted it, even emphasized it in its growing attempts to establish its separate identity and its claim to equal status with schooling. The division between education and adult education constitutes a very neglected obstacle in the way of achieving lifelong learning.*

The definition arrived at by the United Nations Educational, Scientific and Cultural Organisation (UNESCO) is, by contrast, a good example of a broader and more 'modern' conceptualization of adult education:

> *The term 'adult education' denotes the entire body of organised educational processes, whatever the content, level, and method, whether formal or otherwise, whether they prolong or replace initial education in schools, colleges, and universities, as well as in apprenticeship, whereby persons regarded as adult by the society to which they belong develop their abilities, enrich their knowledge, improve their technical or professional qualifications, or turn them in a new direction and bring about changes in their attitudes and behaviour in the two-fold perspective of full personal development and participation in balanced and independent social, economic and cultural development.*

This definition may be compared with that given by another international body, the Organization for Economic Cooperation and Development (OECD):

> *Adult Education refers to any learning activity or programme deliberately designed by a providing agent to satisfy any learning need or interest that may be experienced at any stage in his or her life by a person who is over the statutory school-leaving age and whose principal activity is no longer in education. Its ambit, thus, spans non-vocational, vocational, general, formal and non-formal studies as well as education with a collective social purpose.*

Each of these definitions can be seen to encompass both training and education, vocational and non-vocational provision, study for qualifications and for its own sake, and educational provision outside expressly educational institutions as well as within. Their separate articulation can be seen as another example of the competition between such international bodies in this area.

The OECD definition is the broader of the two, stated in terms of learning activities rather than educational processes. While the UNESCO definition may be equated with post-initial education, the OECD's appears equivalent to post-compulsory education. The former stresses the joint purposes of national and individual development, and can be seen as relevant to developing as well as developed countries. It also neatly avoids the problem of defining what it means to be an adult, by contextualizing it in terms of local societal perceptions.

The widespread use of the term continuing education developed in the United Kingdom partly in response to the perceived restrictiveness of narrower interpretations of adult education, to which it may be seen as an alternative. It is also used partly in recognition of the changing audiences and curricula within education for adults. Thus university Departments of Adult Education, or Extra-mural Studies– the equivalent of extension or external departments in other countries have over the last two decades changed their titles to Adult and Continuing Education, or just Continuing

Education (and again, more recently, to Lifelong Learning or Education). Yet, as with adult education, there are broader and more restrictive definitions of the term in use.

The articulation of a wider role for continuing education can be seen in the work of the Advisory Council for Adult and Continuing Education (ACACE) during the late 1970s and early 1980s. In their major report, the ACACE noted that:

> *Our definition of continuing education is a broad one. We do not think that it is useful to draw artificial boundaries between education and training, between vocational and general education, or between formal and informal systems of provision. We include systematic learning wherever it takes place: in libraries, in the work place, at home, in community groups and in educational institutions.*

This definition would include the whole of further and higher education, in addition to a great variety of provision outside educational institutions, and much that took place outside institutions altogether. It may be contrasted with the very narrow approach to the concept at one time taken by the British government, which saw continuing education in contrast to its non-vocational view of adult education as being confined to post-experience vocational provision for those in employment. This would place its focus on mainly short and non-award-bearing courses, designed to update those working in professional, industrial or commercial contexts.

The broader conceptualization of continuing education gained wider acceptance within the United Kingdom during the 1980s and 1990s, coining to be seen as one of the main roles of both further and higher education institutions. The usage of the term also extended to other, particularly anglophone, countries. For some, however, the term remained reactive rather than radical, lacking either the sense of tradition attached to adult education or the activist edge of community education: 'the concept appears to be a politically neutral one neither making reference or criticism of the initial education system nor implying any form of evaluation of the total contemporary educational system'.

Now, however, continuing education is in the process of being supplanted by the broader notion of lifelong learning, a trend which has gathered pace both nationally and internationally since the mid-1990s.

COMMUNITY

Community education offers a place and space for the 'voice' that is a crucial part of participation and active citizenship.

'Community' is one of those evocative words which sounds innately appealing and worthwhile, conjuring up images of warmth, belonging and place, yet is difficult to pin down as a useful or meaningful concept. Like some of the other concepts discussed in this book, enterprise, it is an ideological, and thus potentially a dangerous, term:

> *'Community' can be the warmly persuasive word to describe an existing set of relationships, or the warmly persuasive word to describe an alternative set of relationships. What is most important, perhaps, is that unlike all other terms of social organisation* (state, nation, society, etc.) *it seems never to be used unfavourably, and never to be given any positive opposing or distinguishing terms.*

A wide range of different meanings for the term 'community' has been identified. Thus, Clark identifies five main points of entry into the idea, viewing community as a human collective, as territory, as shared activities, as close-knit relationships, or as sentiment. Similarly, Newman gives six common ways of interpreting the concept: community as the working class, as the quiescent poor, as the disadvantaged, as the 'whole community', as the acceptable community, and as society. He concludes that:

> *There is probably no single, satisfactory definition of 'community'. But we misunderstand the word grossly if we appeal to the community as any kind of incontrovertible authority, as if we assume that the community can be represented by a single cause. One of the clues to the meaning of 'community' lies in its utter lack of any statutory authority.*

These varied interpretations have not, however, prevented the widespread use of the concept, in education and training as in other fields, in many different countries in both the developed and developing worlds. In some countries, particularly in Latin America and Eastern Europe, the terms popular education and folk education may be used instead of, or in conjunction with, community education. In others, especially developing countries, non-formal education may be the preferred expression.

Naturally, these varied uses have different institutional expressions. Community colleges, for example, exist on both sides of the Atlantic, but the term is applied to different kinds of institutions. In the United States and Canada, community colleges are in the higher education sector, and offer sub-degree and degree-level study. Their nearest English equivalent would, therefore, be a further education college, outside the higher education sector.

In England, community colleges are far less widespread, but generally take the form of secondary schools which offer a range of adult education and recreational provision as well. In Scotland, the term community education is used more generally to refer to adult education, usually offered in association with youth and other community services. The common theme shared by these different institutional forms is their concern to recruit and serve a wide range of people: a community, though not necessarily the whole community.

The use of the term for educational purposes extends far beyond these examples, and has a lengthy history:

> *A survey of twentieth-century developments appears to reveal three major strands in the evolution of community education in Britain. First, the secondary school-based village/community college movement pioneered by Henry Morris in Cambridge shire; second, the trend towards community primary schooling in some urban areas following the Plowden Report and experimentation in the Educational Priority Areas; third, innovative work in adult education and community development undertaken in some of the Home Office sponsored Community Development Projects in the late 1960s and early 1970s.*

The first of these strands relates partly to the examples just discussed, of the community college and the community school. Like many other longer-standing movements, this 'school' of community education has its saints-Henry Morris in England, Charles Mott in the United States-its literature and its advocates. 'Community education is normally understood as the process of transforming schools and colleges into educational and recreational centres for all ages'.

The second in so far as it relates to adult education and training and third strands identified by Martin embody the ideas of outreach and activism. Outreach is concerned with taking educational provision to where its clients are, that is outside of established educational institutions; while activism sees the educator's role as clearly political. The third strand, in particular, links to a more radical 'tradition' of adult education, which sees educators as being the servants of the disadvantaged, and adult education as being about engendering change.

Lovett himself has identified three main approaches within this strand, all of them explicitly linked to serving the working class:

> *There are three distinct 'models' of community education which reflect very different views about the nature of the problems facing the working class and the policies and strategies necessary to resolve them* Community Organisation *usually implies appointing outreach workers to work outside adult education institutions in working class communities. This model is in fact an extension of the liberal tradition in adult education.* Community Development...*takes a more active attitude. Community educators operate in local communities working on various local projects providing information, resources, advice and, when the occasion arises, research, education and training.* Community Action *places greater stress on learning through doing. There is more emphasis on the role of conflict in the resolution of local problems and the opportunities this provides for raising consciousness amongst those involved.*

Lovett's own commitment is clearly to the last of these models, which demonstrates the strongest identification with, and commitment to, working-class communities. It also recognizes that any given community is unlikely to share a homogeneous view on a given issue. Communities, in other words, are groups that are not indifferent to each other's interests, but which are likely to contain conflicting interests.

Amidst all of these types, strands and models, what, if any, common themes may be identified? Another analyst, working within the Scottish tradition, has suggested the following:

Community Education:

1. is a life-long activity;
2. ...that lays great emphasis upon the learner's active participation in learning and decision-making;
3. ...that lays great stress upon the problems and needs of people as starting points for learning...
4. ... that can be identified as being based within identifiable communities whether these be neighbourhoods or communities of interest...
5. ...that lays great stress upon the process of change as well as the achievement of change in itself...
6. is education yet claims to encompass more informal and non-formal methods and contexts.

This definition makes clear the links between community education and the concepts of lifelong education and non-formal and informal education.

Reduced to these common conditions, however, there may seem little implied by community education that is not included within adult education, or within education in general. The ideas of learner participation, starting from the problems and needs of the learner, and educating for change, are found in many contemporary approaches to learning and education. Once the idea of community itself is broadened to apply to either an area or a common interest, most of the remaining distinctions seem to vanish, and with them goes a lot of the warmth and commitment carried by the concept as well.

FORMAL, NON-FORMAL AND INFORMAL

The notions of non-formal and informal education came to prominence during the 1960s and 1970s in international discussions on education, at the same time as lifelong education first became fashionable. Yet, whereas the latter concept has to do with the extension of education and learning throughout life, the former are about recognizing the importance of education, learning and training which takes place outside recognized specialist educational institutions.

In this trilogy, 'Formal education is that provided by the education and training system set up or sponsored by the state for those express purposes'. The other two concepts, non-formal and informal education, were introduced with particular reference to the problems of developing countries. They are, however, also applicable to developed countries, though in such cases they are more likely to be labelled as community education.

In developing countries, the formal educational system will typically only be available to, and/or used by the minority of the adult population. In such circumstances, non-formal education, which encompasses all organized educational or training activity outside of the formal education system, may offer a cheaper and more accessible means for delivering needed learning. Non-formal education, while not constituting a parallel system, covers:

> *Any organised, systematic, educational activity, carried on outside the framework of the formal system, to provide selected types of learning to particular subgroups in the population, adults as well as children. Thus defined nonformal education includes, for example, agricultural extension and farmer training programmes, adult literacy programmes, occupational skill training given outside the formal system, youth clubs with substantial educational purposes, and various community programmes of instruction in health, nutrition, family planning, cooperatives, and the like.*

A simpler definition has, however, been offered by the OECD: 'education for which none of the learners is enrolled or registered'. This stresses the location of non-formal education outside of educational institutions. There, it takes place under the auspices of organizations that do not need to adopt the more restrictive frameworks and accreditation systems of the formal sector.

The advantages of non-formal over formal education for contributing to national and personal development have been stressed:

> *In the context of new development strategies, non-formal education is being viewed as more relevant to the needs of the population, especially for those in the rural areas working in the traditional sector, since it attempts to focus on teaching people to improve their basic level of subsistence and their standards of nutrition and general health. Further, since the non-formal education process usually requires the participation of its recipients in determining the nature and content of the educational programmes, these will always tend to focus on the needs and priorities of the communities.*

Seen in these terms, non-formal education has clear linkages not just with ideas of community education, but more particularly with the practices of educators such as Freire.

The third member of the trilogy considered in this section, informal education, may then be seen to cover all forms of learning not included in formal and non-formal education. Thus, it refers to:

> *The life-long process by which every individual acquires and accumulates knowledge, skills, attitudes and insights from daily experiences and exposure to the environment-at home, at work, at play: from the example and attitudes of family and friends; from travel, reading newspapers and books; or by listening to the radio or viewing films or television. Generally, informal education is unorganised, unsystematic and even unintentional at times, yet it accounts for the great bulk of any person's total lifetime learning including that of even a highly 'schooled' person.*

Here, there are close connections to the ideas of experiential, problem-based, independent and self-directed learning. Recent research in this area has focused particularly on the role of informal learning in the workplace.

Informal learning fits very well with new forms of work organisation and new types of management, and has the potential effect of breaking the power of the formal education system'.

TENSIONS, TRADITIONS AND DICHOTOMIES

One theme is that of tension. Thus, there are evident tensions between the institutional expressions of concepts and the concepts themselves. The labels adult and community, to take two examples, are used differently by different institutions. There are also related tensions between institutional practices and the legal frameworks within which they operate, as exemplified in the overlaps between further and higher education.

Then there are the tensions between institutional forms and individual needs, such that particular adults may be using the same institutions at different ages and for varied reasons. All of these tensions have both spatial, in that usage varies from place to place and country to country, and temporal dimensions, in that the application of concepts has changed historically, as well.

A recognition of this variation provides a useful link to a second theme, that of 'tradition'. This word has been put in single quotation marks not to signify its status as another concept, but to suggest the need for some caution in its use. For traditions are manufactured every day, and it is frequently the case that, when we refer to certain practices as being traditional, they are not of any great historical provenance.

Both adult education and community education have been referred to in this chapter as having traditional interpretations. In these cases, both concepts do have a lengthy history, and their traditions have a basis in historical practices. The point, however, is that, in recognizing and referring back to such traditions, we are really seeking to compare current practices with an idealized version of what once was. This is, of course, a source of further tension.

A third and final theme harks back to the discussion in the introduction of this chapter, and has to do with the relations between the various institutional forms of adult education and training and those for child and youth education. These were expressed in terms of four dichotomies: compulsory/post-compulsory, initial/post-initial, secondary/post-secondary and school/post-school.

The existence of four such dichotomies is evidence enough of the problems in drawing a clear boundary between adult and non-adult education and training. Taken together, they indicate the existence of inevitable overlaps in institutional forms–most evident in England in further education colleges, in North America in community colleges. We might, therefore, conclude that any attempt to neatly delimit a field of adult education and training, the subject of this book, is doomed to failure. Or we might, more positively, argue that it is better to think in terms of an overarching concept such as lifelong education, encompassing all forms and levels of education throughout life.

❑❑❑

6

Conceptual Understandings of Adult Education

INTRODUCTION

The relationship between concepts in adult education and training and five broad themes will be considered. These five themes are not, of course, the only ones which could have been chosen for examination, but they are arguably amongst the most general in terms of application and relevance. They include two themes, time and space *i.e.* the historical and comparative dimensions that were anticipated in the Introduction. The three other themes chosen-policy, theory and ideals have arisen from the analyses presented in the chapters that followed.

TIME

All of the concepts that have been examined in this book like all thoughts, ideas and constructs are located in time. They all have a history. Even where this seems to be brief, there are the connections with other concepts of longer standing to be considered. There are a number of obvious implications which arise from this location in time, but it is surprising just how often these are overlooked, and how frequently individuals seem to believe that they are advocating 'new' concepts.

Because concepts are located in time, they are subject to change and development. There are few ideas that remain constant in their expression for any length of time. Looking back, we may think that we can identify 'traditions', or we may have them presented to us by others. Even these traditions, however, represent processes rather than constancies, and are subject to continual reinterpretation.

Similarly, we can detect fashions in conceptual development and usage. Concepts have a 'sell-by date'. They may rise to prominence, be widely talked about, analysed and applied, only to sink into relative obscurity within comparatively few years. Or they move from the conceptual realm to become the basis of policy and/or be taken as 'fact'.

These changes are not simply one way; in other words, concepts do not just rise, fall and disappear from usage. They are often reused or recycled once or more throughout their history, sometimes wittingly, at other times unconsciously. This may or may not involve a change in the wording of the concept, or perhaps even the complete substitution of one concept for another of essentially the same meaning.

SPACE

Clearly, space complements time as the other obvious dimension in which to understand the location of concepts. Just as the application and meaning of concepts varies throughout history, and has its own history, so conceptual usage and understanding differs from place to place, and country to country. It has an international or comparative dimension.

These spatial variations in conceptual usage can be partly traced, of course, to differences in language and culture. Thus, as has been stressed a number of times in the text, the focus in this book has been primarily on anglophone concepts those which have developed in the English and American systems in particular. Other linguistic and cultural traditions, such as the francophone, have produced and used rather different series of concepts, though in many cases these are analogous.

Yet we live in an increasingly internationalized world and in some ways our ideas and practices are coming closer and closer together. Or, at least, our understanding of others' ideas and practices is improving. Hence, particularly with the post-war rise in the influence of a range of international organizations, many more concepts are coming to have global application and meaning.

POLICY

All governments, political parties and interest groups make widespread use of concepts. Indeed, it could be said that concepts are central to politics, whether driven by ideological concerns or more pragmatic policy-making interests. Concepts offer convenient and superficially simple labels for more complex ideas, which can then be sold to voters or used to rally supporters.

This is not to say that politicians or policy-makers actually create concepts themselves; this rarely seems to be the case. What tends to happen is that they adopt and adapt concepts which are available, and which appear to connect with the ideas and policies they are working with. The meaning and application of these concepts may then be changed quite radically, as in the case of continuing education. A new vocabulary for presenting and analysing them may also be developed.

Where concepts are being used politically in these ways, they will tend to become the subject of much broader discussion and debate. They may then enter popular discussion, rather than being limited to academic or political circles, and be further developed as a result.

THEORY

Concepts also have a close linkage with our ways of furthering our understanding of our world. They can provide a focus for research and theory development. They are used to encapsulate our ideas about what is particularly important or significant in any one area of interest. They offer a means to both organize and explain our concerns.

This is why it is so important for those who routinely handle concepts to have a better understanding of their meaning and application. Offering such an understanding is, of course, the fundamental purpose of this book. Without a broader and deeper view, it would be so easy to interpret concepts solely from one's own, inevitably relatively narrow, perspective.

Concepts also have an important enabling function so far as theory development and research are concerned. Labelling a set of issues or ideas as a concept effectively legitimates, and to some extent demarcates, them as an area for investigation. This is a key way by which disciplinary knowledge develops.

IDEALS

Just as concepts may be linked to ideology by way of their role in politics, so they may be connected with ideals. Ideals and ideology are closely related terms, of course, and may in practice be closely linked with each other. Here, however, the term 'ideals' is being used in a broader and less political sense, for concepts may be presented as ideals or ideal types to be aimed for, as hopeful aspirations, or even as Utopias.

In this sense, some concepts represent unreal and unachievable ideas. Their status as ideals does not necessarily mean, however, that they are of no practical value. They may offer a model or target against which progress and practice may be judged, even if it can never be totally emulated. Concepts may be a process rather than a product. As such, they can have a valid, inspirational role.

In a similar way, some concepts may encapsulate an ideal which is not so much unachievable as ill-defined. In such cases, the concept's role may be to stimulate concern and direct attention. A detailed and pragmatic working out of what the concept may mean in a given context and situation may then follow, which can then allow it to be better achieved in practice.

CONCEPTUAL CHARACTERISTICS

In addition to sharing varied relations with the themes of time, space, policy, theory and ideals, as just discussed, all of the concepts in adult education and training analysed in this book have other characteristics in common. These relate to the concepts themselves rather than their contexts. Three key characteristics will be briefly considered in this section: the tendency of concepts to exhibit tensions, their competitive status, and their positioning within dimensions.

TENSIONS

Part of the role of concepts could be said to be about the recognition and structuring of tensions between differing ideas or perspectives. These tensions exist both within and between the concepts themselves.

An example of the latter would be the varied use of cognate ideas like distance, open and flexible education, learning or training. In this case, it is not altogether clear which is the most general concept, to what extent they duplicate each other, and how best they might be seen as related. We might, for example, view distance learning as either a precursor or a part of open learning. Open and flexible learning, on the other hand, both seem equally all-encompassing, and might be seen as synonymous.

Interestingly, each of these three concepts also presupposes the existence of a paired but opposed 'shadow' concept. The term 'shadow' concept is used, since these are rarely articulated as such, or at least not to the same extent. These shadow concepts we might call respectively face-to-face, closed and inflexible education, learning or training.

For an example of tensions within a concept, the notions of development and success may be used. In the case of development, there is an internal tension between personal and economic interpretations of the concept. In the case of success, there are tensions between simple completion and other possible measures, such that the concept may be interpreted in myriad and individual ways.

Distance education Open learning Flexible training	Face-to-face education Closed learning Inflexible training
Development	Stasis
Community	Conflict
Knowledge	Ignorance
Access	Exclusion

Fig. 6.1. Concepts and shadow concepts

This review of tensions illustrates other common conceptual characteristics. Thus, instead of having somewhat hidden shadows, they may be set up as dichotomies. Examples include education/training and teaching/learning. In some cases, the distinctions being made may be more than two-fold: for example, the three-fold 'trichotomy' formal/nonformal/informal.

Hence, while concepts perform the function of encapsulating important ideas, they are also about making divisions and distinctions. They have a dual role of inclusion and exclusion. From this point of view, it may be equally as useful to be able to say that something is not, for example, education, as it is to be able to confirm that it is.

COMPETITION

The discussion of tensions within and between concepts slides naturally into recognition, in many cases, of their competitive status. Various gradations may be recognized here. Thus, there may be competitive views taken of the same concept.

Competition can also be seen as occurring between concepts that occupy much the same area of discussion, as in the case of experiential and self-directed. Or it may be that similar concepts are deliberately advanced by organizations or interests to compete with each other.

In many cases, including those just instanced, such competition is a partial and temporary phenomenon. After all, the advocates of competing concepts of these kinds will tend to share much the same ideas, and favour similar responses to the same issues. After a period of more overt competition, therefore, the use of such concepts may become mutually reinforcing and supportive, such that their meaning and application may be almost indistinguishable to subsequent generations or audiences.

There are other instances, however, where the competition between concepts is more deep-rooted and thus longer lasting. Here, the concepts are being used to label, advance and contest alternative perspectives of the whole field, and the debate has continued for many decades.

DIMENSIONS

In practice, of course, the position is usually rather more complicated than that. People rarely advocate only vocational education, or only liberal education; or, if they do, they tend to be using the terms in a more general and inclusive fashion. Courses are neither wholly open nor wholly closed.

Such concepts represent positions on a continuum, spectrum or dimension.

Thus, open-closed offers one dimension and also, as already suggested, a dichotomy for judging educational provision or learning experiences. This is a dimension on which all practical examples would be located away from the extreme poles of wholly open and wholly closed. Similarly, any example of education, learning or training is likely to mix elements of the vocational and liberal approaches.

Once we recognize the positioning of concepts along a variety of possible dimensions, it becomes easier to appreciate how they may overlap in certain areas, slide into each other, or even substitute one for the other. Thus, while in many instances it may be relatively easy to justify why we view a given example as education or learning, or as further rather than higher education; in other cases we might not be so sure. Though concepts may be about exclusion as well as inclusion, and may be presented as competitive terms or dichotomies, their boundaries are not necessarily precise, and are subject to perception, negotiation, interpretation and change.

CONCEPTUAL ANALYSES

The discussion so far, in the preceding chapters as well as in this one, has indicated a range of different ways in which concepts in adult education and training may be considered and analysed. The purpose of this section is to look at three particular ways (or groups of ways) by which conceptual analysis might be approached. These are in terms of underlying social variables, organizational levels or educational linkages. The first two of these methods were suggested in the Introduction.

SOCIAL VARIABLES

The consideration of underlying social variables, *e.g.* gender, race, class, age, etc. in the analysis of any issue is at the heart of the social science approach. It is just as valid in the analysis of the use of concepts. In the case of gender, for example, we have seen how the interpretation of concepts like career and skill and indeed of any work-related concept, is rooted in our varying ideas of the roles and positions of men and women in society. A conventional view might equate work with full-time, continuing and paid employment, and thus take an implicitly male perspective. Other, broader views, building on the work of feminist authors, are, however, possible, useful and revealing.

The issue of age, to take a second example, underpins all discussion about adult education and training, at least implicitly. The very field of adult education and training itself is, after all, defined in distinction from child and/or youth education and training. Though adulthood constitutes the greater part of most of our lives, at least in the industrialized world, it is still quite possible to discuss adults as if they were a homogeneous group, and this is a tendency that has to be guarded against.

Age, or more broadly time, is, however, explicit in many of the concepts which have been examined; including, for example, development, lifelong, continuing, career and experiential. These encapsulate the idea of changes during the adult's lifespan.

ORGANIZATIONAL LEVELS

Many of the concepts discussed in this book may be considered in terms of different organizational levels or statuses. The three-fold categorization most commonly used has been that which recognizes the levels of the individual, the organization and the society. This typology may, however, be modified and added to.

We might think in terms of the group or the community, as well as the organization, as lying between the individual and societal levels. The descriptors local, regional, national and international (or global) could be used as an alternative classification, usefully bringing in a recognition of the role of governments and states, as well as of the comparative element.

Some of the concepts that have been reviewed relate only or chiefly to just one of these levels. Thus the learning organization refers primarily to the organizational level, while the learning society is concerned with the societal level. Other concepts can be interpreted at two levels. For example, career may be seen from the perspective of the individual or of the organization, while human capital may be interpreted at the individual or societal level.

In other cases, it is possible, and indeed sensible, to analyse single concepts or series of concepts at a variety of levels. The ideas of access and participation, for example, may each be approached from the point of view of the individual learner, of the educational or employing organization, and of society as a whole.

Alternatively, a series of concepts may enable an analysis of a linked succession of organizational levels. This is perhaps clearest in the case of the international concepts already referred to: lifelong learning, the learning organization, the learning society. These can be seen as articulating shared concern at, respectively, the individual, organizational and societal levels of analysis.

EDUCATIONAL LINKAGES

As the discussion of age in the sub-section on social variables above has already indicated, it is difficult to proceed far in an analysis of concepts in adult education and training without referring to non-adult, that is child and youth, education and training. This is partly a question of definition, and partly a matter of linkage between these two broad areas.

There is, of course, no clear and absolute division between adult and non-adult forms of education and training. This was shown in the analysis of the terms post-compulsory, post-initial, post-secondary and post-school. Adulthood cannot be defined solely in terms of age and there are too many overlaps in provision and practice between adult and non-adult education and training. So there are inevitably some shared concerns that extend across the porous and indefinite boundaries we manage to recognize.

The linkages are, however, much stronger and more complex than that. Non-adult and adult forms of education and training are arranged in a sequential fashion, even if there are gaps, so that almost all of those involved as participants as adults will have also participated as children and youths. The nature of adult education and training is, therefore, largely a reaction or response to what is provided for children. It may take the form of supplementary education, intended to overcome deficiencies in child or youth learning. Or it may be progressional, building upon and extending what has already been learned. Whichever the case, those involved in delivering or understanding adult education and training cannot afford to ignore developments in child and youth provision.

CONCEPTUAL PASTS AND FUTURES

In this final section, two tasks will be attempted. First, looking backwards, I (and here the first person intervenes for the first time since the Introduction) will reflect a little upon what has changed in the conceptual world in the half a decade or so since I wrote the first edition of this book: see also the section on 'what's new about the second edition?' in the Introduction. Second, looking forwards, I will speculate a little about the possible future development of concepts in adult education and training, at the same time reviewing what I said about this in the first edition.

First, then, what has changed since the first edition, written in late 1995 and published in 1996? The major change seems to have been political and policy related. With the change of government in the United Kingdom in 1997,

New Labour or Third Way notions have come to prominence in discussions of education and training, and similar trends can be identified in many other western, industrialized nations. Thus, the emphasis on social capital and social inclusion, both included in this edition for the first time, and the reemphasis on lifelong learning and the learning society, which, in 1995/96, seemed to be of more importance in an historical context. Other changes, however, have been more practical or theoretical in nature. Here I would include the growth of interest in the idea of communities of practice and the increasing popularity of problem-based learning. We may also note the resurgence of interest in the nature of knowledge, evidenced both in the concept of knowledge management and in the debate about types or modes of knowledge. By implication, however, not much has changed since the first edition of the book was produced. Indeed, all of the concepts discussed then, with the sole exception of recurrent education (now subsumed by lifelong education and rarely mentioned), are still included in this edition. However, it is possible to identify some concepts that have declined in popularity. These would include:

- the idea of continuing education, now overrun by the more contemporary notion of lifelong education;
- the concepts of andragogy and conscientization, which may now be seen as part of the history of adult education and training; and
- the notions of capability and enterprise, which now sound like last decade's slogans, even if much of their content is still contained in more contemporary labels.

Second, what of the future? In the first edition of this book, I stated that I would expect many of the following conceptual developments to take place in the future:

1. A continuing recycling, reinterpretation and renaming of many existing concepts. A fairly safe prediction to make, but it has been borne out and I would expect it to continue to be.

2. A continuation of the vocational/liberal tension in conceptual discussions, with the emphasis moving back some way towards the liberal perspective at some point in the not too distant future. This debate seems likely to be with us forever, but I do not yet detect much movement back towards the liberal perspective (too hopeful perhaps?).
3. A good deal of conceptual activity, stimulated by the growing policy debate, around the ideas of the learning organization and the learning society. This has definitely been a major area of conceptual activity during the last five years, though the learning organization may be being overtaken by the notion of knowledge management now. Similarly, the interest in the learning society has been paralleled by the resurgence of interest in the notion of lifelong education.
4. The development and popularization of additional concepts to do with further, higher, adult and continuing education and training; reflecting both the expansion and diversification of these areas of provision. This is evident in the increasing attention given to, for example, problem-based learning and modes of knowledge.
5. A growth in the area of work-related concepts, building upon the increasing prevalence of linkages between education and work. Definitely a major area of interest, as seen in the continuing attention paid to human capital and the rise of social capital as a concept.
6. The effective rejection of the idea of andragogy, and its replacement by other proto-theories to explain and understand adult education and training. I think we are still waiting for developments here.
7. Considerable activity around the concepts of competence and quality, to better define and critically assess their meanings and application. This has happened, at a detailed, practical level.

8. Further work on the ideas of success and failure, and outcomes, to more adequately recognize the multiple routes that are possible through and beyond education and training. There have been some developments here, but more is needed.

Overall, then, a fairly accurate set of predictions, though the details have differed from what I might have expected. My other specific prediction, or rather hope, was for the development of a new concept of 'learnership'. This concept was seen as referring to two aspects of adult education and training. First, it would recognize the active and continuing engagement of certain adults in learning, both over a considerable period of time and in a range of different settings. Second, it would reinforce these adults' recognition of this activity as an important, valid, related and integral engagement alongside other major life roles like worker, parent and partner. On this prediction, though I can detect some developments *e.g.* in terms of policy, the government introduced the ill-fated notion of Individual Learning Accounts; while, in terms of analysis, there has been some exploration of the related idea of learning careers I think more are due.

Finally, do I have any new predictions? I do have one major one, and, in a sense, it is one that I missed last time. This is that the arena of adult education and training and the concepts within it will become more and more politicized. I think this will happen at two levels. Most obviously, at the national (and, of course, international) level, where adult education and training has become a major concern of government. But also, however, and more insidiously, at the institutional level, whether this be an educational institution or an employer in a more general sense. Here, the increased attention being paid to adult education and training will have a practical, and frequently compulsory, impact.

7

Developing the Curriculum for Adult Education

INTRODUCTION

Curriculum development, which is concerned with the aims, processes and outcomes of educational provision, has become an area of increasing importance within adult education and training over the last few decades. Two main, linked reasons for this may be identified: the overall rise in levels of provision and participation, and the increased interest taken by the government and other external authorities in the nature of the education and training being delivered. What is taught, and how it is taught, are currently seen as being issues of more general concern, and not to be left to individual teachers or lecturers, their employers or institutions.

As in the case of many of the other areas considered in this book, there is an extensive range of concepts in use, of which only some will be analysed here. The term curriculum is itself, of course, a concept of note. It is one which has been extensively discussed from a school-based perspective, though less so by adult educators. There are a number of tensions evident within these discussions between differing views of the curriculum:

- curriculum as an area of study (i.e. a syllabus) or all of an educational institution's activities;
- curriculum as content, product or process; and
- the formal, informal and hidden elements of the curriculum.

The approach taken in this chapter will be both broad, in its interpretation of the scope of the curriculum, and selective, in its choice of concepts for examination. The emphasis will be on overall approaches to the curriculum, rather than particular aspects of its planning, delivery or evaluation. The chapter starts with what may be seen as the more 'traditional' concepts of knowledge and skill. These concepts can be seen to underpin all adult education and training, as well as embodying some of the opposition evident between education and training.

Though by no means new, they have come into, or back into, prominence during the last two decades. These concepts are those of competence, capability, enterprise and quality. They share the characteristic of resulting largely from the intervention within education and training of outside interests.

KNOWLEDGE AND SKILL

Type A knowledge is defined in terms of propositional knowledge, codified and stored in publications, libraries, databases, etc., subject to quality control by editors and peer review, and given foundational status by incorporation into examinations and qualifications. Under this definition, skills are regarded as separate from knowledge. Type B knowledge is defined in terms of personal knowledge *i.e.* what people bring to practical situations that enables them to think and perform. Such personal knowledge is acquired not only through the use of public knowledge but is also constructed from personal experience and reflection. It includes propositional knowledge along with procedural and process knowledge, tacit knowledge, and experiential knowledge in episodic memory. Under this definition, skills are treated as part of knowledge rather than as separate from it.

The concepts of knowledge and skill have a long history and a widespread common usage, and, as Eraut suggests, are inextricably linked together. As already suggested, they can also be seen as representative of the perceived dichotomy between education and training. They are not, of course, the only such oppositional terms. With a little thought, a list can readily be compiled.

education	*versus*	training
knowledge	*versus*	skill
understanding	*versus*	experience
theory	*versus*	practice
academic	*versus*	vocational

Fig. 7.1. Conceptual dichotomies

To take this presentation a little further, the latter (right hand) of each pair can be seen as useful, public, external and to do with the 'real' world, while the former may be caricatured as useless, elitist, internal and within the ivory tower. Such caricatures are only such, of course, and fall down as soon as any more detailed analysis is engaged in. Yet, they do have purchase and influence, and are not so far away from being the views of many of those with power to influence education and training.

What, then, is meant by knowledge? More absolutist and objective conceptions of knowledge are still, of course, adhered to by many, particularly those coming from a background in the pure sciences. Others, including the present author, lean towards more relativistic and changing perceptions. This is not to deny the power of science, however, or its general view of its subject matter as potentially entirely knowable, but to recognize that such an approach does not work from all disciplinary perspectives. Sociologists, for example, will typically see knowledge, like truth, as socially constructed. Many philosophers see it as inseparably connected with power:

> *Knowledge, therefore, does not simply represent the truth of what is but, rather, constitutes what is taken to be true*

Thus, rather than taking changes in knowledge as the progressive unfolding of truth, it is necessary to examine the complex exercise of power which is immanent in such changes.

Much recent research and writing on knowledge seeks to distinguish between different types of knowledge. Thus, in the quote that opens this section, Eraut distinguishes between propositional knowledge which might be characterized as academic and factual and personal knowledge, that which is held and used by individuals. He further divides the latter to include not just elements of propositional knowledge, but also procedural, process, tacit and experiential knowledge. In earlier research on managers, he identified six types of knowledge: situational, people, practice, conceptual, process and control; which, he claimed, might be generally applicable, at least to other professions.

An alternative perspective on, and categorization of, knowledge starts from the recognition that the 'traditional' producers and assessors of propositional knowledge, the universities, are under increasing challenge from other institutions and groups (e.g. private companies, community groups). This situation is seen as being particularly competitive at a time when the possession and development of useful knowledge is of increasing importance:

> *The parallel expansion in the number of potential knowledge producers on the supply side and the expansion of the requirement of specialist*

knowledge on the demand side are creating the conditions for the emergence of a new mode of knowledge production.

As a consequence, it is argued, there are now two main kinds of knowledge:

By contrast with traditional knowledge, which we will call Mode 1, generated within a disciplinary, primarily cognitive, context; Mode 2 knowledge is created in broader, transdisciplinary social and economic contexts. The emergence of Mode 2 is profound and calls into question the adequacy of familiar knowledge producing institutions, whether universities, government research establishments, or corporate laboratories in Mode 1 problems are set and solved in a context governed by the, largely academic, interests of a specific community. By contrast, Mode 2 knowledge is carried out in a context of application.

These kinds of arguments are currently both popular and influential (see also Nowotny, Scott and Gibbons 2001). However, they do not seem to be saying more (indeed, it could be argued they are saying less, or are saying something rather different) than Eraut and others have been saying for some time, and in a more measured way.

The notion of skill also presents problems with different disciplinary definitions and interests:

Labour economists generally see skill as a property of an individual, made up of various combinations of education, training and competence. Industrial sociologists, on the other hand, have normally regarded skill as an aspect of jobs themselves, derived from the imperatives of industrial and technological organisation, without giving much attention to the relations between the skill of jobs and the skill of people Social historians have focused predominantly on the skilled divide within the manual working class and particularly on the role of apprenticed craftsmen in the development of trade unionism. There is, therefore, no shared conception of skill amongst social scientists. The concept is both multi-valent and complex.

Yet, while recognizing these differences, we can go further than this. One analyst, for example, working from a comparison of the professional and amateur approaches to painting a room, has identified five main characteristics of skill: fluency, rapidity, automaticity, simultaneity and knowledge. Another author presents a somewhat similar listing:

There are four criteria for the application of the term 'skill':

1. a situation of some complexity;
2. a performance that addresses the situation is deliberate and is not just a matter of chance;
3. an assessment that the performance has met the demands of the situation;
4. a sense that the performance was commendable.

Unlike the previous listing, this formulation does not specify, but implies, the existence of some relevant knowledge.

From these analyses we can detect some of the problems with applying the concept. For it is not just multi-valent but multi-level: we can use the same term to talk about an international concert pianist and our local plumber. Not surprisingly, it is with the latter that most concerns are raised namely, how to increase the skill levels of the working population in order to enable us to better compete in the global economy.

This interest, coupled with the recognition that neither education nor work is for life, has led to the recent concern with developing what have been called personal transferable skills. Developed in the initial period of education, and refined through continuing education and training, such generic skills are supposed to make workers more flexible, adaptable and able to learn. Personal transferable skills are at the heart of the capability and enterprise initiatives, discussed in the next section, and are also central to the competency movement, the subject of the section after that.

Before leaving the concept of skill, however, we should recognize that, like knowledge and other concepts, it is both socially constructed and a political term. The degree to which a performance is regarded as commendable, to use Barnett's words, is a matter of perception, and that perception crucially depends upon status: the status accorded to the performer and the performance, and the status of the person making the judgement. Hence, the concert pianist is likely to be regarded by most people as more skilful than your local plumber.

Since issues of power and status are involved, skill also has a crucial gender component: 'the classification of women's jobs as unskilled and men's jobs as skilled or semi-skilled frequently bears little relation to the actual amount of training or ability required for them. Skill definitions are saturated with sexual bias'.

These views are linked to perceptions of paid and unpaid work, and to the varied interpretations of career. There are clear implications here for changing patterns of work: 'Feminisation of a particular occupation or profession is seen to have the effect of deskilling it'. School-teaching, for example, particularly at primary level, might be seen as an illustrative case of this process in operation.

CAPABILITY AND ENTERPRISE

Capability and enterprise are two concepts that came to prominence in the United Kingdom in the 1980s and 1990s. They do, however, have a longer history and more general meanings, and have also been similarly applied to education and training in other countries. While they could not be said to be as influential now as they were a decade ago, their development and application is still of interest, as it tells us much about the use of concepts for politics and policy.

While there are similarities between these two concepts, there were key differences in their promotion and in the level of resourcing behind them. Capability was a slogan launched by the Royal Society of Arts, a body concerned to bring together educators and industrialists, and advance their joint interests. Enterprise, on the other hand, was one of the key concepts underlying the thinking of the Conservative governments of the period, and heavily funded through the Manpower Services Commission and its successor bodies. Whether either concept has had a lasting impact of itself (as opposed, that is, to contributing to underlying trends) on the education and training landscape would be a matter for debate.

It was a characteristic of both of these initiatives that neither of the promoting bodies saw a pressing need to define what they were talking about, or seeking to encourage, with any precision. It was left, at least initially, to those seeking funding or support through the initiatives to interpret what the promoters were after. This was sometimes excused on the grounds of the difficulty of definition:

Capability does not lend itself to detailed definition. It is easier to recognise it than to measure it with any precision. It is an integration of confidence in one's knowledge, skills, self-esteem and values. Capable people have confidence in their ability to – (1) take effective and appropriate action, (2) explain what they are about, (3) live and work effectively with others, and (4) continue to learn from their experiences, both as individuals and in association with others, in a diverse and changing society.

As this quotation indicates, however, the early reluctance to be precise was soon supplanted by a quite detailed, though not necessarily particularly helpful, formulation. What is given here is a very general definition of some of the desirable qualities of fellow workers or citizens. There are not many hints as to what a 'capability curriculum' might look like, nor as to how it might differ from learning activities lacking that conceptual heading.

This lack of precision did not, however, prevent a broad mixture of educators and industrialists from endorsing the Education for Capability movement. Nor did it stop the officers of that movement from visiting and recognizing courses or programmes as developing capability in their students. Not surprisingly, these processes themselves led to the identification of some common features. Thus, the leaders of the Higher Education for Capability offshoot of the movement came to recognize four themes:

- reviewing and building upon previous experience, knowledge and skills;
- preparing plans and negotiating approvals;
- active and interactive learning;
- the assessment of performance according to agreed learning outcomes.

The enterprise initiative may be seen to have been more narrowly focused than the capability movement. Its concern was with the development of just work, rather than work and life skills. The Conservative governments of the 1980s and 1990s were responsible for launching and funding a whole raft of enterprise schemes. These covered the themes of employment and unemployment, education and training. They ranged in their targets across the lifespan from schoolchildren to older adults, though youths were the key target. Among these schemes were, for example, the Technical and Vocational Education Initiative, the Enterprise Allowance Scheme, Enterprise in Higher Education, Enterprise Awareness in Teacher Education and even Evangelical Enterprise in Higher Education (EHE), to take just one example, was launched in 1987, and promised one million pounds each to higher education institutions which were prepared to embed enterprise throughout their curricula. As in the case of the capability movement, enterprise was not initially defined, but it was clearly implicit that only applications endorsing the Manpower Services Commission's particular view of enterprise would receive funding. Within a year of the launch, the sponsors, now renamed as the Training Agency, had become more explicit:

As well as being qualified in a particular discipline, students who have attended a course which includes enterprise will:

- have a positive attitude towards enterprise activity;
- have developed personal transferable enterprise skills;

- be better informed about employment opportunities, aims and challenges and make better career choices;
- be better prepared to contribute to and to take responsibility in their professional and working lives.

Tensions can be identified within this statement between the development of 'skills' and the inculcation of 'attitudes' (as they similarly can be in the reference to values in the capability definition quoted). Some have seen this as tantamount to suggesting a process of indoctrination to make students more favourably disposed towards enterprise. The vocational focus was transparently obvious, and most EHE programmes duly involved local employers in the planning, delivery and even assessment of courses, and developed 'realistic' project work and placement schemes. Bids for funding identified a limited range of personal transferable skills that would be developed in students, typically including problem-solving, group work and presentational skills.

With a further year's experience of the programme, the Training Agency was ready to reflect back to its educational audience the implicit and explicit meanings of the concept that they had identified:

There are many definitions of 'enterprise'. Definitions may focus on:

- **Entrepreneurship:** The qualities and skills which enable people to succeed in business enterprises;
- **Personal effectiveness:** The qualities and skills possessed by the resourceful individual;
- **Transferable skills:** The generic capabilities which allow people to succeed in a wide range of different tasks and jobs.

A reasoned assessment of the Enterprise in Higher Education initiative would be that it has had at best modest success, in terms of getting academics to think about and implement both curriculum and staff development. Both the concept and its implementation were heavily criticized. For some this critique was based on what was seen as unwarranted government interference, for others on a challenge to the traditions of liberal education, and for still others on the perceived inability of employers to make effective use of recruits with enterprise skills.

More generally, the whole movement for embedding industrial values within education, of which the capability and enterprise schemes can be seen as parts, has been ably deconstructed by Coffield:

> *We are not dealing with a tightly defined, agreed and unitary concept but with a 'farrago' of hurrah words like 'creativity', 'initiative' and 'leadership' some notions which are central to most definitions of enterprise, problem-solving for instance, have been taken from psychology and then simplified, decontextualised and invested with a significance and power which few psychologists would be prepared to support the potential terms of reference of words like 'capability' or 'skills' (or 'enterprise') are so wide that to call someone 'capable' or 'skilful' (or 'enterprising') without specific context is meaningless enterprise tends to be viewed as an individual attribute and both structural factors and local economic conditions are ignored where is the independent and convincing evidence of the success of enterprise education or enterprise initiatives?*

The problem with capability and enterprise is not just that they are so self-evidently, in the applications discussed here, transient buzz-words, lacking in hard, analytical credibility; but in the assumptions that they make about educators and trainers, their employers and their clients. These groups are seen simultaneously as sharing common aims and being highly malleable. That the commonality of their aims might be only apparent at a general and simplistic level, disguising an underlying and possibly healthy diversity of practice, is not seen as important, provided that they can be persuaded or cajoled into endorsing and operating common approaches.

The capability and enterprise movements may thus be seen as expressions of a fundamental lack of trust in British education and training institutions and providers. The drive towards competency-based education and training, the subject of the next section, may be viewed in a similar fashion, though it differs in terms of both its overall scope and the degree of control imposed. In that sense, it represents a further development of the desire to centralize influence and control over a recalcitrant educational service.

COMPETENCE

Like many changes in social policy, the idea of competency-based education and training was transferred to Britain from the USA. The spur for its application was the perceived lack of relevance of existing vocational provision and the need to compete better with other economies:

> *One of the growing concerns amongst employers has been that much of the provision of VET [vocational education and training] was not seen as being directly relevant to the needs of employment...it was considered that VET tended to be 'educationally' oriented both in content and the values which are implicit in its delivery. It has tended to concentrate on the acquisition of knowledge and theory while neglecting performance, and it is performance which essentially characterizes competence.*

In response, the British government set up a Working Party on Vocational Qualifications, which reported in 1986. It defined its core interests in the following terms:

> *A vocational qualification is a statement of competence clearly relevant to work and intended to facilitate entry into, or progression in, employment, further education and training, issued by a recognized body to an individual. This statement of competence should incorporate the assessment of:*
>
> - *skills to specified standards;*
> - *relevant knowledge and understanding;*
> - *the ability to use skills and to apply knowledge and understanding to the performance of relevant tasks.*

Competence itself was defined later on in the report as 'the ability to perform a particular activity to a prescribed standard'. This framework was quickly accepted by the government of the day, and a National Council for Vocational

Qualifications (NCVQ) was established to oversee the rapid introduction of National Vocational Qualifications (NVQs), and later General National Vocational Qualifications (GNVQs), throughout education and training.

The introduction of a national competence-based education and training (CBET) system was welcomed in some quarters as providing a positive challenge:

> *CBET has a constructive effect on some long-held assumptions about designing and assessing learning programmes. It confronts the unthinking acceptance of institution-bound, formal, time-served programmes, and raises questions about whether traditional forms of assessment really do address the learning outcomes teachers claim to promote.*

These challenges included the identification of what competences actually measured, and what they did not:

- *Competence is concerned with what people can do rather than with what they know.* This has several implications:
- *firstly* if competence is concerned with doing then it must have a *context.*
- *secondly* competence is an *outcome*: it describes what someone can do. It does not describe the learning process which the individual has undergone.
- *thirdly* in order to measure reliably someone's ability to do something, there must be clearly defined and widely accessible *standards* through which performance is measured and accredited;
- *fourthly* competence is a measure of what someone can do *at a particular point in time.*

The issue of what UDACE referred to as 'context', and the Working Party described as 'relevant knowledge and understanding', was clearly also of critical importance. Hence it became necessary to identify not only the specific competences required and tested for, but also what became known as their 'underpinning' knowledge and understanding. When this was taken into account, the idea of competence could be talked of in rather broader terms, and might be seen as little removed from, or as a successor to, the concepts of capability and enterprise.

One of the problems with CBET, though, is that the concept of competence continues to be articulated and used in a variety of ways:

One can distinguish four different ways of conceptualising core competences:

1. Metacompetence or metacognitive skills, i.e. the intellectual skills involved in competent learning and problem solving.
2. Basic competences or core skills, i.e. the core body of knowledge and skills that must be learned as a foundation for all other learning.
3. Integrated model of competency: the ability to act within an organisation which is dependent on the holistic integration of technical, methodological, social and behavioural competences.
4. Organisationally embedded competency: the outcome from the interaction between skills, technical infrastructure, roles and organisational social system.

At whatever level it has been conceived, however, the concept and the policy have attracted a good deal of criticism. One of the earlier published critiques noted that:

> *The idea of assessing through the use of competence statements and associated performance criteria is superficially attractive since it appears to guarantee a certain level of ability which may be expected to be transferable from the specific situation in which it was acquired. However the competence notion has been stretched too far we believe that 'competence' is the embodiment of a mechanistic, technically-oriented way of thinking which is normally inappropriate to the description of human action, or the facilitation of the training of human beings.*

Or, as a more recent critic has put it, rather more trenchantly: 'Competency-based standards are not so much a metaphor for technical-rationalism but more a set of tools used by technical-rationalism to disguise and make more palatable some of its operations'. Others have attacked the policy as imprecise, confused, reductionist and applicable only to certain lower-level skills or activities: 'these aims are basic minimum, lowest common denominator ones, and leave just about everything else to be said about VET, adult and higher education'.

These criticisms suggest a linkage between the concept of competence and higher-levels of skill and performance, reflected in the notions of professionalism and expertise, which may be seen as being beyond 'mere' competence. This link is made explicit in the Dreyfus model of skill acquisition, which recognizes five successive stages: novice, advanced beginner, competent, proficient and expert. The distinction between the two concepts is spelt out in Benner's application of the Dreyfus model to nursing:

> *Competence, typified by the nurse who has been on the job in the same or similar situations two to three years, develops when the nurse begins to see his or her actions in terms of long-range goals or plans of which he or she is consciously aware. The expert performer no longer relies on an analytic principle (rule, guideline, maxim) to connect his or her understanding of the situation to an appropriate action.*

In other words, experts can perceive large and meaningful patterns in their domains of expertise, and they have deeper levels of understanding. Given the level and range of criticism that has been levelled at the competency movement, it may seem somewhat surprising that it has been so widely adopted within education and training, both in Britain and elsewhere:

> *It is somewhat remarkable that the considerable critical response levelled at the competence approach in recent years has done little to prevent the spread of CBET into almost every area of contemporary educational discourse in the UK. The case against CBET is certainly formidable the behaviouristic and reductionistic failings of the approach are well-known but what makes the unremitting advance of CBET perhaps all the more remarkable is the manner in which its advocates have seemed able effectively to side-step theoretical censure.*

A number of possible explanations for this success may be advanced. One is that the vocal critics of CBET are a relatively small minority, and that most practitioners of education and training, punch-drunk from decades of policy change and only too aware of the weakness of their changed contractual position, are just seeking to get on with their jobs. Another would be that the advocates of CBET have effectively colonized the ongoing concerns and debates of educators and trainers:

> *Student-centred learning, negotiation of individual learning programmes, the accreditation of prior learning, the valuing of non-educational and training institutions as sites of learning, the need for guidance and counselling of learners; all of these now form an essential part of the discourse of competence. In other words, the dichotomy of 'traditional' and 'progressive' educational discourse is elided. It is precisely through its articulation with liberal humanist ideas that discourses of competence are powerful, not simply within the formal structures of education and training, but, more important, over and through learners.*

QUALITY

While the focus on the quality of education and training provision has been contemporaneous with the introduction of competency-based systems, the former concern has been much more international in its scope. It can also be seen as impacting upon all levels of provision, from school through further education and university to professional and continuing education.

The model for quality that has been advocated, with government support, since the 1980s has been that of the successful private company, with the mechanisms for ensuring quality in education and training being largely taken, with little adaptation, from manufacturing industry:

> *We now have a plethora of custodians of quality, all of whom are at least to some extent legitimated by the Education Reform Act of 1988, the Further and Higher Education Act of 1992 as well as the White Paper with its concerns for quality and accountability. The latter,*

particularly, not only referred to levels of quality assurance: quality control, validation and examination, and external assessment, but also specifically mentioned quality systems-BS5750 and Total Quality Management (TQM).

In addition to quality assurance, control, validation, examination and assessment, reference may also be found to quality audit, management, enhancement, circles and improvement teams. As well as the British Standard BS 5750 and other national standards, there is an International Standard ISO 9000; and, within the United Kingdom, there are related schemes such as Investors in People and the Management Charter Initiative. These techniques and standards have been applied throughout the public, private and voluntary sectors, and not just in the areas of education and training.

It would not be too far-fetched to say that, in a very short space of time, a quality industry has grown up within British education and training. It is an industry with competing branches, and one that is placing an increasing bureaucratic load on those responsible for the actual delivery of education and training.

Amidst all of this activity, however, relatively little attention has been given to just what might be meant by quality, and to whether it has distinct characteristics in an educational context. It is, after all, commonplace to hear statements along the lines of 'I don't know what quality is, but I know it when I see it'. After all, quality, like standards, is a concept or principle with which it is very difficult to disagree. While this does not excuse us from our task, it is as well to recognize the difficulties and the resonances attached to words like 'quality':

Quality, like 'freedom' or 'justice', is an elusive concept. We all have an instinctive understanding of what it means but it is difficult to articulate. Quality is also a value-laden term: it is subjectively associated with that which is good and worthwhile.

Quality is also a contested concept that embodies tensions within itself, such as those between:

- the demands of external accountability and the processes of internal improvement;
- the idea of a gold standard and of something that is 'merely' fit for its purpose;
- criterion and norm referencing (i.e. do we judge quality in terms of some absolute standard or with reference to our competitors?);
- assessment of inputs and/or outputs, or of the whole educational or training process;
- cross-disciplinary or discipline-specific demands;
- responsive or strategic approaches.

There are two answers which are not necessarily incompatible with each other. The first focuses on *processes*, the second on *outcomes*. Process-based quality assurance relies on observation of teaching and learning and the activities that support it. Inspection is the most common form of process quality assurance. Outcome-based quality assurance relies on the *assessment* of the outcomes against certain pre-agreed standards. Examination and testing are the most common forms.

Ultimately, of course, it is difficult to see how anyone could ever be entirely satisfied with the quality of anything, be it an artifact or a service. We could always potentially do better. So there is no end to quality assurance and assessment. Seen in this light, the current concern with quality-like the capability, enterprise and competence movements-is in large part to do with control.

A POLITICAL BATTLEGROUND

We can identify tensions within the concepts themselves. If we call someone skilful, capable, enterprising or competent, are we saying something banal or praiseworthy? Are these minimal or acceptable standards? How can they be measured or assessed? These tensions can even be detected, though to a lesser extent, in the concepts of knowledge and quality. If, for example, we refer to something as everyday knowledge, we may, depending upon our perspective, be dismissing it as commonplace or holding it up as of value.

Second, the interrelationships between the concepts analysed are close and complex, involving opposition and overlap. It is common to find advocates of one concept decrying another, reflecting the continuing dissonance between the core concepts of education and training. Yet it is also common to see the concepts identified defined in terms of, as well as in relation to, each other. The closer the analysis, the more skill slides into knowledge and the nearer competence comes to understanding.

Third, this conceptual battleground is also, and perhaps primarily, a political battleground. Underlying the debates reviewed here is a fundamental challenge to the professionalism of educators, trainers and their institutions. This challenge is coming from policy-makers and hinders who are convinced that our vocational education and training systems have not been delivering what is required of them, to the detriment of the competitiveness of the economy. Hence we are not just dealing with concepts here, but also with slogans and their supporting ideologies.

The idea of curriculum is hardly new but the way we understand and theorize it has altered over the years and there remains considerable dispute as to meaning. It has its origins in the running. It was, literally, a course. In Latin curriculum was a racing chariot; currere was to run. A useful starting point for us here might be the definition offered by John Kerr and taken up by Vic Kelly in his standard work on the subject. Kerr defines curriculum as, 'All the learning which is planned and guided by the school, whether it is carried on in groups or individually, inside or outside the school. This gives us some basis to move on and for the moment all we need to do is highlight two of the key features:

- **Learning is planned and guided.** We have to specify in advance what we are seeking to achieve and how we are to go about it.

- **The definition refers to schooling.** We should recognize that our current appreciation of curriculum theory and practice emerged in the school and in relation to other schooling ideas such as subject and lesson.

In what follows we are going to look at four ways of approaching curriculum theory and practice:

1. Curriculum as a body of knowledge to be transmitted.
2. Curriculum as an attempt to achieve certain ends in students - product.
3. Curriculum as process.
4. Curriculum as praxis.

❑❑❑

8

Organizing Community for Adult Education

INTRODUCTION

People face many problems that can be solved through collective action. They experience feelings of helplessness when they lack knowledge about what can be done. Key to community organizing are identifying a problem or issue and providing sufficient information about the problem and about options available to resolve the problem. Mobilizing people to join collective efforts requires motivation and participation. The motivation may come from an individual's perception that only through group action can the problem be solved. Participation requires that residents see the problem as personal and perceive themselves in some cases as victims concerned about improving their lives. Through a series of mini-successes with collective action, community organizations give people the confidence they need to resolve many of their most serious problems. Organizing the community for learning and action is a people-oriented process, designed to establish group identity and to promote social change for the betterment of the people.

ORGANIZING GOALS

Community organizing as it is related to community development has five goals, which reflect the direction and substantive elements of a systematic process. The first goal is to increase the potential of individuals to participate. Second is to create an atmosphere of participatory democracy. The third is to provide an opportunity for learning and problem solving. Fourth is to enhance local empowerment. The fifth is to establish an on going vehicle for community development.

INCREASING THE POTENTIAL OF INDIVIDUALS

The most immediate effects of organizing start with individuals by targeting them as an important resource that is needed for service to the community. People can fulfil the need to be involved and to expand their knowledge base about problems and issues affecting the community. Community organizations offer many residents a new opportunity for accomplishment, for excitement, and for a sense of belonging by expanding horizontal relationships with neighbours. For people who have limited life experiences and education, community organizations can inspire them to enhance their potential for a fuller participation in the life of the community.

CREATING AN ATMOSPHERE OF PARTICIPATORY DEMOCRACY

An insistence upon democratic values is a precondition underlying the ideology of community development. According to **Boyte**, the democratic thrust represents a sincere faith in citizens that given the information and means, people can make important decisions about all aspects of their lives. "In turn, the building blocks for a revitalized ethos of citizenship are to be found in the voluntary structures of all kinds at the base of American society". To carry out the democratic ideal, the leadership of the community-organizing effort must be ever mindful of creating and preserving this fundamental condition.

PROVIDING OPPORTUNITY FOR LEARNING AND PROBLEM SOLVING

The development of the community starts with the development of individuals, providing them with knowledge about themselves, their group, and the environment. Learning is viewed as a connecting process of understanding states of tension (problems), examining them, and investigating ways of arriving at a resolution. This involves choosing actions for problem solving. Group problem solving requires group consensus on the definition of the problem.

ENHANCING LOCAL EMPOWERMENT

Empowerment represents the increased capacity of local citizens to make and control decisions that affect their lives. In the context of community development it means decisions directly related to the life and vitality of a neighbourhood, including activities and projects initiated and operated by citizens. Empowerment also refers to the ability to influence prevailing government and political systems to achieve goals of the community. Central to empowerment is the local leadership's willingness to confront and challenge formal authority through creative techniques, which give them the advantage.

ESTABLISHING AN ONGOING VEHICLE FOR COMMUNITY DEVELOPMENT

Community development, from a locally controlled perspective, is facilitated when citizens form their own organizations to provide for the community the long-term capability and capacity to bring about community improvement. Within community organizations there may be occasional units that have a relatively short life cycle for example, a campaign to influence government education authorities to build and support a local library for the community. Generally, the local umbrella organization should be established for a long-term existence.

PRINCIPLES AND PROCEDURES OF ORGANIZING

The impetus for organizing may come from two or more people in a neighbourhood who are concerned about a common problem. Gradually, more people are persuaded to join the core group as they perceive the need to do something about the problem. The organizing effort must concentrate on significant, broad-based community issues if a mass base is to be achieved. Early in the process, there is a need for an educational effort so that citizens can be informed about the facts of an issue or concern. If such a need is neglected, people will drop out, and the organizing will fail. Alinsky provides a set of principles that form the rationale for mass organizing that focuses on an appeal to the self-interest of residents to secure something they want. Alinsky's ideas of the essential factors of effective community organization are summarized by Rose as follows:

(1) The organization must recognize self-interest as its raison d'être, but to be effective it must aim at a multiplicity of goals. It should attract and involve most of the groups in the community.

(2) In order to create self-respect through success, the program must be specific, immediate and feasible.

(3) The organization must choose its means on the basis of the means that are available and likely to be most effective, and

(4) it must recognize and accept the factor that controversy has always been the "seed of creation" and that it is inevitable that resentment will focus on the prevailing dominant interest of the status quo.

In assisting Mexican-Americans to organize in 1953, **Alinsky** provided a sketch of the following principles:

1. You must work *with* people rather than for people.
2. It is not enough to work on a particular problem; you must also get after those persons who caused the problem, or who can help solve the problem.
3. The resident of a community is more concerned with his/her own problems than is anyone from the outside.
4. Given the opportunity, local residents can and must do the job; no one else can do it for them.
5. The American way of life is to feel that you "belong."
6. When the sources responsible for a problem have been identified, it is important they maintain steady pressure on them until the problem is resolved.
7. To improve ones situation, more is needed than just a cause. To get something from politicians, voting power is required, which implies a mass-base organization.
8. The organizing effort must concentrate on bread-and-butter issues if a mass-base is to be achieved.
9. If people "don't want" something, it may well be because their past experience may convince them that the situation is hopeless. Therefore, it is essential to achieve some visible success quickly in order to sustain hope in the people.
10. Effective leadership can be found at any level.

An organization based on the foregoing principles is oriented to action to resolve a serious deficiency or injustice. Alinsky frequently advocated confrontation strategies as a means of resolving problems that reflect long-standing injustices found in most minority American communities. During the 1950s and 1960s, confrontational methods were also the principal tools of civil rights activists. However, given the decline of many historic injustices in America during the past twenty years, there has been a perceptible shifting from confrontation methods to self-help methods of community development.

BOOTSTRAPPING

A contemporary neighbourhood linear organizing strategy is known as bootstrapping. This is a step-by-step approach to building a neighbourhood or community organization. A guiding principle at the early stage of bootstrapping is that the group should start with a small project that will succeed so that it will experience achievement and develop a sense of confidence in collective action. Rubin emphasize that immediate success can become an incentive for more people to get involved in the organization.

Bootstrapping represents two distinct stages. The first stage involves an activity that has little input from community residents, but yields a victory. For example, community residents sign a petition for street sweeping, and the city responds positively. Subsequently, people perceive that they have acquired power as a result of their collective actions. The identification of a winnable issue by powerless people taught them something about empowerment.

The second stage of the bootstrapping process requires that community residents, with their newly found group confidence, move from small successes to larger and more complicated issues. To bootstrap successfully at the second stage, organizers must continue to choose issues that offer a high probability of success. Building the community organization for a long-term struggle requires that the horizontal relationships among residents become strengthened for the purposes of solidarity and unity. Here, the focus is on the *process*, rather than the *content*. Once people feel they are members of a community with a sense of belongingness, the resistance to participation is reduced. Strengthening horizontal relationships can also be beneficial for sustaining collective awareness during periods of inactivity and then allowing for immediate mobilization when collective action is required.

The bootstrapping process of community organizing is based on a step-by-step sequence of procedures. **Cunningham** and **Kotler** provide a typical set of steps as follows:

1. A crisis or an organizer's initiative provokes a few people.
2. This determined handful forms the beginning cadre.
3. The cadre defines the exact nature of the issue to be worked on and begins to move.
4. Additional members are recruited as efforts on the issue pick up steam.
5. The cadre and followers achieve some success on the issue and seek outside allies if needed.
6. The cadre and others involved move to form a permanent organization, choosing to build the structure from either existing organizations or individual members.
7. The new organization evolves a strategy: it will get things done by putting pressure on government and other targets, or it will provide services to people, or even try to do both.
8. The new organization picks an additional issue or two, building power, utilizing cooperation, campaigning, and confrontation as appropriate.
9. Members are trained to be more effective.
10. Regular communication is established with members and with the public.
11. A stable source of income is developed, but no more than needed.
12. Alliances are made with other organizations as useful.
13. Evaluation is made a habit.
14. Recruiting new members and facing new issues go on continuously.

ORGANIZING *VS.* DEVELOPING

The primary approach to community problem solving involves organizing and educating residents in order to influence decisions that affect their neighbourhood. The organizing effort is basically issue-oriented advocacy. On the other hand, *development* is a substantive step beyond *organizing.* Some writers in the community development literature emphasize a dichotomy between organizing and developing. For example, in *organizing,* residents of a neighbourhood may come together to support an important issue or concern. The *organizing* neighbourhood will then lobby or pressure the appropriate officials for results. On the other hand, in *development,* residents of a neighbourhood will move beyond issue support and pressure, taking the direct responsibility for planning, implementing, and operating a *development project.*

Many community organizations stress the need to engage in organizing as the principal means by which to impact and control improvement and revitalization efforts. These organizations tend to avoid direct development involvement because of the perception that it may have negative repercussions for the organizing and advocacy initiatives of the group. In this sense, development is viewed as a highly technical and time-consuming enterprise, which may derail or diminish the organizing activity. The loss of the constituency is the major fear. Issue-oriented community groups rely on their ability to influence public policy and a variety of externally controlled development agencies that provide services to their neighbourhood. These types of community organizations are prevalent in middle-class affluent neighbourhoods.

Many community structures reflect organizing and development components. Some of these organizations originally addressed only neighbourhood issues, but over a period of time they were expanded to involve development activities. There is no inherent conflict between these components, but rather a management problem of providing a proper balance between the two. Kolodny provides a succinct analysis regarding community groups that move from organizing into development. There are some tensions that can result between the two components of organizing and development. Fundamentally, development requires much greater capital resources. Such resources can rarely be accumulated by the collection of membership fees and community fund raising. The costs of development projects include the hiring of technical staff. These projects must acquire external funding (and technical assistance), which is both complex and time-consuming. At the same time, there is the danger of diverting attention away from the organizing effort. This may weaken the base of citizen support for development. Organizers worry that citizens may become passive in speaking out on controversial issues involving public and private agencies, particularly if these agencies represent actual or potential funding sources. In order to combat these and other tensions, community groups must employ a number of creative approaches that achieve a proper balance of organizing and development so that overall progress can be made.

Despite the tension between organizing and development, there are many benefits to community groups involved in the dual components. The first is that the group can fill the void in a situation where no agency is able or willing to take on a particular development project. A second benefit is that this approach ensures that the development meets the community's needs. Two other important benefits are the acquisition of ownership of the development product (buildings, equipment, etc.) and the building of local skills and competencies for self-sufficiency.

THE ORGANIZER

Community organizing as a process is initiated and carried out by individuals. These individuals range from residents of the neighbourhood undergoing organization to individuals who reside outside that neighbourhood. A key individual is required in the early stages of establishing and building the community organization. This individual may be referred to as the *organizer*. The literature uses different labels to refer to the organizer: *community developer, change agent, encourager, development agent,* and *nucleus-level worker*. Although there may be minor distinctions among the different labels, essentially they should be considered synonymous. In the past, organizers tended to be professional agents attached to a formal institution or agency. Most of today's organizers are nonprofessionals who reside in the particular community being organized. The community development literature over the years has consistently emphasized three dimensions relative to the community organizer: roles of the organizer, personal qualities needed, and training experiences.

ORGANIZER'S ROLES

Fundamentally, the organizer is viewed as the instigator of the community development process. The organizer may have a special skill or expertise in an academic area, but this may not be related to the organizer's internal motivation to community activism. Frequently, organizers represent individuals who are dissatisfied with some social issue and understand why people do not act, or why they reflect feelings of powerlessness. The individual organizer develops a belief that social issues can be resolved through the collective action of neighbours. Primarily, the community organizer is concerned with bringing people together to induce change in their community, but at the same time the organizer is devising the process in a democratic manner so that people will realize the possibility of empowerment. The recognition of social change built around visual signs of community improvement has a concomitant profound psychological impact on residents.

Community organizers come in all sizes and shapes. A variety of leadership and management styles characterize the spectrum of community organizers. One's philosophy, particular expertise, and experience play an important role in determining the tasks that an organizer may emphasize. Given the differences that characterize nonprofessional and professional organizers, there are several dimensions that provide clarification in attempting to understand the types of community organizers. One dimension involves identifying the *basic approach* to organizing and development. The specific elements are enabling, facilitating, assisting, teaching, and brokering. Organizers, depending on their management style and other factors, may utilize and reflect two or more of the basic approach *elements* in the performance of their roles.

Morris provides a simple typology of community agents, based on the main tasks performed by agents: the field agent, the advisor or consultant, the advocate, and the planner.

The *field agent* is the individual who is the street-level worker. This agent is in immediate and continuous contact with neighbourhood residents. Being aware of the neighbourhood history and cultural values of the people is an essential requirement for this agent. This agent must be sufficiently knowledgeable about the ideas and workings of the larger society so as to serve as a link between expressed local needs and external resources. Important information from residents is gathered through dialogue, rather than coercion or intimidation. The principal problems for this agent are maintaining objectivity, translating expressed needs into realistic expectations, and interfacing with appropriate external agencies.

The *advisor* or *consultant* has expertise in a technical area related to the specific needs of a neighbourhood. This agent may know very little about the socio-cultural context of the community and is usually connected through employment to an external agency. This agent relies on the field agent and other local functionaries to translate and pinpoint expressed needs. The preliminary advice may take the form of educating community residents relative to specific services or interventions that are available and appropriate for local utilization. The advisor also must be able to confirm and negotiate local analyses to decision makers at external agencies.

The *advocate* plays an important role as the link between the neighbourhood and the "establishment." Advocacy requires a deep commitment to the needs and aspirations of residents in the neighbourhood. Advocates must be able to suppress their own views in favor of expressing and promoting those views of the group. Frequently advocates perceive themselves as representing those who are not currently empowered or articulate enough to speak for themselves. The primary goal of the advocacy effort is to bring attention to a neighbourhood issue and hopefully to start a process of receiving a favorable response toward the ultimate resolution of that issue. Advocacy may start with individuals, but as the group is energized, it becomes a ubiquitous process.

The *planner* is an invaluable resource person who plays a major role in the development scheme. Development planners require a combination of skills, drawn first from those of the field agent, advisor, and advocate. The planner is primarily a "technocrat" who understands the necessity of being able to translate community needs and wants into some kind of technical plan. In this capacity, the planner must be knowledgeable about the extent to which internal and external resources might be mobilized for a development plan. Given the contemporary trend of self-help community development, planners must be able to identify tasks and skills that relate to community participation and involvement in the planning and operation of projects.

DILEMMAS, PITFALLS AND PERSONAL TRAITS

Community organizers, whether they sum the process or the task orientation of community development, face certain predictable contradictory situations in attempting to fulfil and maintain specific role definitions. As a central figure in mobilizing community residents to achieve certain goals, organizers must work for the prominence of others instead of themselves. Most professional organizers face an initial dilemma, which results from their bondage to professionalization and a concomitant desire to be of service to the residents. These two allegiances may sometimes be in conflict. If the organizer has direct links to an agency, the element of institutionalization enters the picture and further compounds the dilemma. Must the organizer follow strict directions from the employing agency? Or community directives? Educators and others from the "helping professions" are particularly susceptible to finding themselves in such dilemmas. All of them must confront and resolve these paradoxes in such a manner that serving the needs of community residents takes precedence.

Organizers and development agents must constantly be aware of the many pitfalls that can diminish or prevent them from achieving the lofty goals of community development. The prominence and empowerment initially attached to agents must be ultimately transferred to residents instead of being retained by the organizer if the long-range goals and the continuity of the organization are to be achieved and maintained. Organizers and development agents who seek to make their work a career frequently fail to transfer prominence.

A common problem faced by many agents is the "do-gooder" mentality. These agents perceive themselves as missionaries with all of the "right" answers. The do-gooders have often decided that the people are too ignorant and unmotivated to help themselves. Therefore, it follows that the do-gooder must provide a welfare approach to problem solving. This behaviour causes frustration for agents because it has a greater likelihood of eliciting negative or passive responses from residents. The agent's emphasis on the community development process can be a favourable means of reducing frustration and increasing the meaningful participation of residents.

A final dilemma involves the agent's use of influence. This is particularly crucial in that the agent's influence is only one voice in a competing chorus of actors, both internal and external to the community. In the midst of these varied influences, the agent must remain calm and objective. Action may be delayed or disrupted, depending on the source of the influence and the complexity of the political dynamics. Nevertheless, the agent must continue to exert influence through others so that steady movement toward goals is facilitated. As favourable changes are recognized, the agent must acknowledge the group's influence instead of seeking self-aggrandizement.

The personal traits of community organizers are important determinants of role definition. A study of trait theory reveals that earlier beliefs emphasized genetics or inborn traits, which were observed in the persona of great leaders. Contemporary theories relative to personality attributes stress a combination of source-genetics, culture, and learning. After some efforts to train community leaders and organizers, Alinsky identified what he considered to be the ideal qualities of community organizers: curiosity, irreverence, imagination, sense of humor, vision of a better world, organized personality, integrated political schizoid, ego, a free and open mind, and political relativity. After years of attempting to train organizers, Alinsky concluded that some of the ideal qualities could not be taught, that students "either had them, or could get them only through a miracle from above or below". Yet, Alinsky continued to train organizers and community leaders, many of whom are engaged in important community development projects today. Alinsky also emphasized the distinction between community leaders and organizers: "The leader goes on to build power to fulfil his desires, to hold and wield power for purposes both social and personal. He wants power himself. The organizer finds his goal in creation of power for others to use".

It is highly desirable that community organizers develop leadership and management styles that reflect bits and pieces of many personal attributes. The value of having a broad base of these attributes is premised on the complexity and variations of situationally related problem-solving issues which are encountered in community organizing and development activities. There is a strong belief that in community organizing and development, history does not repeat itself! Therefore, any specific learned patterns of problem solving can only be useful conceptually and generally. The chances for problem-solving replication are few and far between. A contingency leadership and management style has the greatest likelihood of success.

CITIZEN ACTION AND ROLES

During the past thirty years there has been an extension of political democracy to new groups and individuals in the United States. This has come about as a result of the civil rights' revolution, women's liberation movement, tenants' organizations, and other group initiatives designed for social change. The extension of the one person-one vote principle to many formerly disenfranchised Americans has broadened the base of democracy. Citizens have demanded a shifting from the concept of representative democracy to one of participatory democracy. More recently, there has been a movement toward neighbourhood democracy. This is characterized increasingly by greater citizen input at the grass-roots level in government policy making, decentralized government services offering better citizen access, and continued formation of a variety of independent citizen groups.

The inclusion of rank-and-file citizens in government and community-based agencies can be viewed as a dual movement in the United States. Langton differentiated this group phenomenon from two perspectives *citizen involvement* and *citizen action*. The former is a government-initiated (top-down) procedure and activity aimed at involving citizens on boards and committees so they share in the decision-making relative to specific public programs. The latter is a community-initiated (bottom-up) procedure and activity employed by common citizens to monitor and influence government policy and program operations. From the community-based development point of view, the citizen action model is particularly relevant.

Citizens can play a variety of roles within the framework of the citizen action model. Actions resulting from these types of groups have led to neighbourhood revitalization, adjusted utility rates, and improved streets, lighting, and sewage systems. Boggs cites citizen coalitions that have emerged to study and confront actions affecting several Ohio communities, "including the hazards of toxic waste disposal, proposals to build and widen highways and plans to raze historical buildings". A significant aspect of a citizen action group's organization and development functions is *education* (i.e., nonformal adult education). Education as a distinct activity is viewed as purposeful and vital to the formulation of action plans. The group's involvement in self-study is placed at a strategic point in the process so as to enhance and sustain group interest and determination.

Boggs provides a description of citizen group research, which examined the five overlapping and sequential stages of the flow of activities: (1) arousal, (2) protest, (3) organization and self-education, community education, and (5) resolution. Stages three and four are devoted to education and represent the two most important and time-consuming stages in the sequence. Stage three provides for a period of self-study, which enables the group to evaluate, synthesize, and focus on specific facts and knowledge to be acquired for an understanding of the community issue. Stage four is an extension of self-education (for the group) to community education for citizens. Stage five employs a number of methods, including public hearings, mass meetings, and speeches at meetings of related groups, agencies, and institutions. Ultimately the purposes of the community education are to allow for input from community residents and to garner public support for the action plans.

Sanders identifies four major personnel roles that citizens play in the operation of the community development process: (1) local leaders, (2) resident professionals, (3) professional organizers (external), and (4) multipurpose workers. The first role places reliance on the participation of local leaders who vary in qualifications, views of the process, and a willingness to devote time and energy to the process. Professionals play an important role in the process by representing a particular specialization (e.g., engineering, education, or the construction trades). The external organizer is a professional who is brought in to perform temporary specific tasks related to the accomplishment of a program or project. Multipurpose workers represent the majority rank-and-file residents who are generalists and perform a variety of required tasks.

Zander suggests that the *roles* citizens play are determined by the nature of their *motivations*. He defines *motive* as "an individual's disposition to strive for a certain kind of satisfaction". Four motives are identified: (1) a self-oriented motive, (2) a desire for group success, (3) a desire to benefit others, and (4) a desire to benefit the community. A self-oriented motive propels the individual toward achievement because of personal incentives. A group success orientation provides satisfaction for teamwork and pride in the group's accomplishments. A desire to benefit others provides satisfaction for accomplishments that are directly beneficial to a target group outside of the organized activist group. A desire to benefit the community is the capacity to accomplish goals that have a common effect of broad community improvement. The willingness, time, and endurance of citizen participation based on motivations are largely an outcome of the intensity and strength with which such motives are psychologically internalized.

THE FOCUS ON LEARNING

The organization and development of a community involves the training, education, and development of individuals. The relationship between community development and adult education can be found within the spectrum of learning about one's self and environment in the process of formulating plans for action. Adult education can be viewed as a process that benefits individuals, while community development can be viewed as a process that benefits a group or community. However, this distinction must be understood in the sense that it is a psychological fallacy to concentrate on individual learning without regard to the role relationship played out in the larger context of the community in which individuals function. From this perspective, adult education may be viewed as a strategy that is concerned with the process and outcome of learning in relation to the betterment of the community. In this sense, adult education is not simply concerned about self-knowledge and self-development of skills and attitudes; it is also an activity that assists people to understand their own potential and to examine ways of alleviating community tensions and resolving problems.

FUNCTIONAL LEARNING

Community development requires a balance in learning relative to the three domains: cognitive (knowledge), affective (attitudes), and psychomotor (skills). Cognitive learning involves knowledge about one's self, one's group, and one's environment. Affective learning consist of onés emotional reactions toward self, others, things, and tasks. Psychomotor learning involves a broad range of skills, including not only motor skills, but also skills in communication and group discussions. Without question, there is a general overlapping of the learning domains, although a particular subject may be *primarily* associated with only one. In focusing on learning in the context of domains, the *process* of adult education is emphasized. The *content* of learning should be chosen as appropriate to facilitate the *functions* of learning. A knowledge of adult learning theories with implicit assumptions provides a framework for understanding some aspects of human development.

Different learning theorists tend to draw different influences from common behaviours and demonstrated relationships. Three theory categories self-determination, humanistic vs. behaviouristic, and andragogy appear to have a more influential relationship with adult education and community development.

Self-Determination. Basic philosophical and clinical techniques developed by Carl Rogers during the 1940s brought about the practice of client-centered therapy. Rogers replicated the basic principles of self-determination and self-direction in the field of teaching. His thinking was based on the major premise that if in therapy it is possible to rely upon the capacity of a client to deal constructively with life's problems and if the therapist's aim is to accommodate that capacity, then why not applies this proposition and this technique to teaching. The undergirding principle of this new teaching method is that it is the teacher's responsibility to encourage and to help nurture the learner's capacity for self-direction and fulfilment. The student-centered approach can be further extended from the teacher to the group leader. The leader establishes the climate for group participation by communicating in many styles reflecting trust in the group. Rogers' principles were adopted by UNESCO many years ago in its annual report *Learning to Be*. In his writings, Abraham Maslow stressed the concept of "self actualization." Maslow emphasizes the expansion of self and the accompanying motivation that propel individuals in an upward spiral in search of the pinnacle self-actualization. Maslow suggests that people can secure a better way of life by striving to produce "self-actualizing behavior."

Humanistic vs. Behavioristic. Although humanistic theories of learning emphasize expressive behaviour and behaviouristic theories emphasize problem-solving behaviour, they are not mutually exclusive. However, when learning activities reflect an emphasis of one or the other of these two positions, methodology is usually different. Contrasting positions involving the use of different teaching methods are discussed in the writings of Bruner and Skinner. Bruner contends that since learning and problem solving depend on the exploration of alternatives, instruction must enable learners to-explore alternative learning modes. On this basis, learners will be able to develop independent skills and confidence in their ability for self-direction. Bruner describes this result as the "autonomy of self-reward." According to **Skinner**, *behaviour is viewed as a product of an individual's interaction with the environment.* To understand the cause of behaviour, investigations must examine prior external circumstances. A major difference in the humanist and behaviorist positions is the recognition of authority and control. While humanistic positions emphasize permissive practices that encourage and support self-direction, behaviouristic positions favor structure, control, and the adherence to certain specifications.

Andragogy. The concept of andragogy espoused by Knowles combines elements of the humanistic and the behavioristic positions. The underlying philosophical assumption of andragogy is that the adult learner has a deep psychological need to be self-directing, and also a vast reservoir of experiences upon which to draw to assist in learning. Andragogy has been scrutinized by many adult education scholars. Cross questions whether andragogy should be considered a theory. She states that "whether andragogy can serve as a foundation for a unifying theory of adult education remains to be seen. It has been far more successful than most theory in getting the attention of practitioners, and it has been moderately successful in sparking debate; it has not been especially successful, however, in stimulating research to test the assumptions".

Knowles further clarifies the notion that andragogy may not exclusively apply to adult learners, but may involve youthful learners in some situations. The andragogical model is based on five assumptions: (1) the self-direction of the learner; (2) the role of learner's experience; (3) a readiness to learn; (4) an orientation to learning; and (5) a motivation to learn. The model is *process*-oriented, as compared with the *content* orientation of the pedagogical model.

There are several unresolved issues that have emerged from an analysis of the application of current learning theories. Whether learning is valued as an intellectual and cognitive process, a motivationally propelled self-actualizing process, or a rational and alternately determined problem-solving process has definite program implications. The application of learning theory must be responsive to the process and programming requirements of adult education for community development. In a practical sense, the democratic process of citizen participation should be enhanced. Situation-based programming is required to respond to identified community needs that can be impacted by educational interventions. The following broad issues of daily life represent a continuum of education needs, which can be addressed through effective programming: civics and politics, economics and social, home and family life, personal growth, aging, workplace and skills, leisure, and environment.

POLITICAL AND PRACTICAL CONSIDERATIONS

Codified learning relative to functional topics is sometimes necessary and helpful, but this learning must also include insights regarding the political nature necessary for the effective utilization of such learning. Many groups of citizens are organized to influence politicians and bureaucrats on a variety of civic matters. Knowledge of and information about a specific civic issue are important, but there are many overarching learning that groups must master if they are to gain access to the decision-making process. For example, the following tips were developed from a citizen participation workshop at the 1987 National Conference on Civic Renewal in Boston:

1. Pin politicians down on their rhetoric. If a council member says "I'm for equity in the allocation of neighbourhood expenditures," that's a commitment for which the person should be held accountable.
2. Develop and promote your own issues. Use creative methods to make an impact.
3. Test out your strategies in the neighbourhood. Rework your issue as necessary.
4. Research how things are done in your area. Avoid offending others or re-inventing the wheel.
5. Narrow your target. Focusing makes it easier to understand and gain support.
6. Building support is a continuous process. Invite local officials to your meetings.
7. Always ask for more than you need. Give government officials the opportunity to compromise.
8. Welcome input from other neighbourhoods. Be cautious in imposing your own views.
9. Know who you are by having a reputable group identity to project.
10. Teamwork pays off. Standardize procedures and representations.

The foregoing tips are learning that recognize the political ramifications inherent in group efforts to influence government officials and politicians. In addition, citizens should be able to identify the important public officials involved in policy decision making. For example, most cities have an annual public hearing on the city budget. The purpose of such a hearing is to allow citizens the opportunity to analyze how well public agencies are performing and to make recommendations for improvement. Before citizens can provide effective testimony and influence the budget process, they should be able to answer the following:

- *Who* are these budget makers?
- *How* do they go about making decisions?
- *What* do they decide?
- *When* do they do so?

Because budgets consist of many complex numbers and tables, many citizens perceive the task of analyzing the budget to a be difficult process and impossible to influence. Yet, examples abound where citizens have learned the technicalities of budget preparation in connection with attendant political considerations. Most of the learning is concerned with how the budget process works, how to get involved, and the importance of reaching the departments before their budget requests are firm.

QUEST FOR EMPOWERMENT

Empowerment is a very important component of community-based development activities. One vital goal of community organizing is to increase citizens' capacity to control certain aspects of their lives through empowerment. Empowerment is a sociopolitical concept that goes beyond notions of participation and consciousness raising. Mere involvement in elections and other periodic civic duties is *not* sufficient because decision making by others on issues affecting their daily lives occurs on a constant basis. Therefore, citizens must be ready to take action at the time when action is required.

In recent years, social movements involving issues of women, minorities, the aged, the handicapped, and other special interest groups all seek the attainment of goals related to empowerment. A comprehensive definition of the operational conceptual framework of empowerment requires the understanding of three important components.

1. **Cognitive.** This component refers to group members understanding of their history, social status, conditions of subordination, and the related reasons for current conditions. It involves an understanding of the conceptual basis of knowledge: What is it? Who has it? How did they get it? Why did they get it? Also, most attention is addressed to legal issues (i.e., human rights and civil rights).
2. **Psychological.** This component involves the understanding of emotional states—feelings, attitudes, and belief systems as they relate to self-esteem. Research suggests that one cannot teach self-confidence and self-esteem to others. However, one can provide certain conditions in which these positive attributes can develop. Educational programs can enhance positive psychological development by treating citizens as participants, rather than beneficiaries.
3. **Economic.** The final component refers to the creation or development of productive activity that will enable citizens to improve their financial condition. These conditions relate to either individual or community. The economic component is particularly important to citizens from low-income communities, the belief being that people will devote their energies to satisfying survival needs before they approach higher-level needs.

Nonformal adult education programs that seek empowerment goals must involve citizens in *all* stages of the program. Some professionals, teachers, doctors, and social workers see their role as planning *for*, instead of planning and working *with*, community residents. This is the single greatest threat to empowerment. Establishing a climate for the growth of empowerment requires that professionals perceive residents as equals. Fried argues that professionals acting as facilitators in community education must learn to relate to people in terms of reciprocity.

Reciprocity is thought to lie at the heart of the question of "empowerment" versus "delivery of service". Professionals who perceive citizens to be ignorant and lazy, and who usually refer to them as "those people," will find it almost impossible to view them as equals. However, those professionals who are conscientious and understand their role in the empowering process have no problem in viewing community residents, regardless of their status, as equals in the exchange of ideas, feelings, and actions. The empowerment process is less a giving of knowledge and information by the professional to the citizens than a partnership. The professional does not become unprofessional because of the sharing process, but rather gains participant status and is perceived as an integral member of the community. This provides a liberating effect for the professional.

Empowerment is not an absolute state of being. There are degrees of empowerment. The more community organizations determine goals, work to accomplish goals, receive benefits from group actions, and evaluate the values of actions and benefits, the more community empowerment exists. However, empowerment as a goal can be very elusive specially if it is pursued and measured by the control of and benefits to a single community organization. In recent years, joint actions among government, communities, and the private sector have brought about local and regional empowerment.

SUMMARY

The discussion emphasized the importance of local participation and the building of community organizations in order to increase the potential of individuals through a collective effort. A discussion of conceptual issues related to principles and procedures of community organizing was provided. Some of the self-explanatory principles associated with the work of Saul Alinsky were listed.

Bootstrapping as an important grass-roots organizing procedure was discussed with particular reference to the various stages of the procedure. A step-by-step sequence of the bootstrapping process was discussed. A careful scrutiny of the process indicated that it starts in simplicity with a rather narrow focus, and, as organizing develops, there is an expansion of factors and goals, including efforts that may be extra-local to the community. A distinction was made between organizing and developing. This was explained in the sense that development usually means acquiring capital, which requires direct management responsibilities for a community organization. This tends to cause tensions among local members when both organizing and development are pursued.

The roles of the organizer and the citizen were explored. Four types of roles of organizers were identified and explained. Role identification, to a large degree, is reflective of the personal attributes and management style of the organizer. The role of the citizen was discussed in the context of differentiated role definitions and motivations for participation.

A discussion of planning with regard to learning concepts of adult education and community development was provided. Political and practical considerations were indicated as an infusionary requirement in bringing about a functional quality to learning. Empowerment as the ideal pinnacle of success was discussed as the ultimate goal.

9

Challenge to Serve Minority Groups in Adult Education

INTRODUCTION

Equal opportunity in education from elementary to university levels has rapidly expanded in the past thirty years for all racial groups and socio-economic strata. However, all national surveys indicate that adult education has failed to serve minority populations proportionately. The reasons for this national tragedy are many. Rosenthal offers two general hypotheses: national efforts to enfranchise minorities increased in the 1960s, with declining action in subsequent years; and during the rapid growth of adult education in the 1970s "those in charge of programs reached out, with no invidious intent, to their most accessible clientele people like themselves who were white, affluent, and well educated". Jones discusses a changing mood in the United States during the 1970s, asserting that the federal government began to shift its emphasis away from social programs and the plight of minorities. She contends that one of the arguments of the neoconservatives was "that

Blacks have made enormous progress since 1964, so no further assistance is necessary; those Blacks who have failed to make it are genetically inferior, lazy".

Adult illiteracy as a national problem resurfaced in the 1980s. Kolenbrander assessed the Reagan administration's policy toward adult illiteracy and found that it was unwilling to provide major new funding and sought to get the business establishment involved in solving the problem. The corporate response was to focus attention on its employees with no involvement among the general public sector. It does not appear that federal or state governments will mount any national or regional programs in the 1990s. Increasingly, minorities are initiating their own programs of adult education and community development. They desperately need assistance from the formal sector of adult education to augment, refine, and expand programs for underserved minority groups.

PERSPECTIVE

Most countries in the world consist of majority and minority populations based on differences of race, ethnicity, religion, and culture. Historically, social theories to promote nationalism often imply that minorities of a given country should undergo a process of acculturation and assimilation into the majority culture. The "melting-pot theory" of the United States was viewed as the requirement for establishing an *American* culture. The concept has been generally effective for those Americans of European ancestry (majority), but has failed for Americans of African, Asian, and Latin American ancestries (minorities). The failure is the result of multiple factors imposed on minorities by the majority. for example, group oppression, racial discrimination, and segregation. Today, the U.S. Constitution, which serves as the "law of the land," has been amended several times to protect and guarantee the rights of freedom and equality to all U.S. citizens. Despite a sound legal structure for an open society, the *de facto* practices of discrimination and bigotry directed toward minority populations continue. In earlier years the practices reflected overt and blatant actions; these have lessened, yielding to practices reflecting covert and institutional actions.

Traditionally, U.S. public education has been viewed as the major vehicle that could acculturate and assimilate minorities into the mainstream. American public education has been under attack since the 1970s for failing to meet the educational needs of minorities. One important criticism focuses on the monocultural nature of the school curricula, which attempt to serve a multicultural population. This has given rise to the principle of "cultural democracy," which requires "the right of every American child to remain identified with his own ethnic, racial, or social group while at the same time exploring mainstream American cultural forms with regard to language, heritage, values, cognition, and motivation".

MINORITY GROUP OVERVIEW

In this chapter the term "minority" refers to three principal groups in the United States: African-Americans (blacks), Mexican-Americans (Chicanos), and Native Americans (Indians). These three minority groups represent about 18 percent of the U.S. population. In June 1990, the U.S. Census Bureau released population counts of 29.9 million blacks, 13.4 million Mexican-Americans, and 1.8 million Indians in the United States. Most African-Americans and Chicanos live in metropolitan areas, and Indians are largely rural residents. The educational needs of these minorities stem from the fact that most of them have not benefited from the public school system compared to the majority population. Minorities are also underrepresented in formal adult education programs. The enrolment of blacks in adult education has been declining in recent years.

The picture has been different with regard to minority participation in nonformal adult education. There has been a long tradition of nonformal education in the African-American community. Sponsors for such programs have included churches, civil rights organizations, fraternities and sororities, parent-teacher organizations, tenant associations, and civic organizations. The success of the programs in increasing participation suggests that the program designs are formulated to reflect social, economic, and cultural values unique to a particular minority community.

During the 1960s, Mexican-Americans in California established a chain of community organizations known as community service organizations (CSOs). The activities of the CSOs varied depending on the need of the local area. For first generation and newly arrived Chicanos, citizenship and English language classes were organized, along with providing political education, obtaining social welfare benefits, organizing farm workers, and bringing public pressure to confront discriminatory practices in the public and private sectors.

Historically, educational programs offered on Indian reservations were designed to Christianize and civilize the residents. Generally, these efforts were met with resistance because they conflicted with deeply held Indian cultural values and customs. The curriculum of the early Christian schools consisted of religion, farming, homemaking, and the three Rs; few Indians completed the programs, and those who did usually left the reservation. The present social and political activism of Native Americans appears to emphasize the need for self-determination and community control of all Indian affairs. This has significant implications for education in general and adult education specifically. Robbins believes that some progress has been made in understanding the problems of Indians and suggests a focus of teaching for "cultural literacy." Cultural literacy "compares and contrasts certain distinct cultural differences as they relate to one another in the total social scheme of American ethnicity".

Minority education needs can be determined partially by examining demographic and other local data. However, these analyses must also be viewed from the perspective of the history and cultural values of each minority population. Caution must be exercised in this process because of the inunroup diversity that is found in all minority groups. Basic definitions for the terms "culture" and "value" are provided, followed by a brief description of important historic and cultural aspects related to the educational needs of the three minority groups.

CULTURE AND VALUE DEFINED

Culture is the totality of socially transmitted behaviour patterns, language, beliefs, values, customs, institutions, and all other products of human activity and thought characteristic of a community or population group.

A *value* is the esteem or importance that is attached to those things that people want, desire, or need in an order of priority. Values serve as the motivation for our action. They are viewed as ideal symbols associated with a specific area, and functionally a value may emerge as a *sentiment*. Behavioural indicators of a value are: "(1) choosing freely; (2) choosing from among alternatives; (3) choosing after thoughtful consideration of the consequences of each of the alternatives; (4) prizing and cherishing; (5) affirming publicly; (6) acting upon choices; and (7) repeating". Minority values, to some extent, reflect a subculture or micro-culture of the majority culture in which they are found. Subcultures are not "lesser" than the predominant culture, nor should they be viewed as "inferior." They are simply different.

AFRICAN-AMERICANS

There can be no understanding of the African-American's plight in the United States without some knowledge about the history of this experience. This history has had a profound effect on the interpersonal relationships between blacks and whites. A comprehensive history of the black experience in the United States remains to be written, but must be portrayed in the words of **James Baldwin**: *"the oppressed and the oppressor are bound together within the same society; they accept the same criteria, they share the same beliefs, they both alike depend on the same reality"*.

HISTORICAL BACKGROUND

Blacks of African descent have been in the Americas for more than 400 years, overlapping six periods of history, which characterize the nature of the black experience in America from 1619 to the present. The first and longest period was *slavery*, which existed for 244 years—from 1619 to 1863. The second period was reconstruction, following the Civil War. The third period was the segregation era. The desegregation era was the fourth period, initiated by the Supreme Court's decision declaring segregated schools unconstitutional in 1954. Desegregation of public schools has been a slow and anticlimatic process. The *fifth* period is referred to as the black revolt era of the 1960s. This period was characterized by civil unrest and violent demonstrations in urban areas across the country. The *sixth* period is the *modern* era, which commenced after passage of the Civil Rights Act of 1964 and the Voting Rights Act of 1965. This major federal legislation was thought to be, at the time, the last hurdle that blacks needed to overcome for full inclusion in American society.

Because of space limitations, the discussion regarding the historical background of African-Americans will cover only the two most recent periods: the black revolt and modern eras. These two periods have tremendous implications for adult education and community development.

The Black Revolt. Black revolts have been recorded during all periods of the black experience in the Americas.

During the postslavery and reconstruction eras the black revolt was centered around organizing protest movements designed to eliminate mob violence, racial discrimination, and segregation in U.S. society. Several national organizations were formed to plan systematic protests, direct-action strategies, and legal redresses. Earlier organizations include the Afro-American Council, National Negro Business League, Niagara Movement, National Association for the Advancement of Colored People, Urban League, and Universal Negro Improvement Association. The Congress of Racial Equality (CORE), officially formed in 1942, was a major organization in the civil rights movement, which began in the 1930s. CORE's main focus was on attacking discrimination in places of public accommodation. The most widely publicized reports of violent black revolts come from those incidents that occurred in the 1960s. "Burn Baby Burn" was the slogan of the radical black activists of this era. During the period 1963 through 1967, major civil disorders were recorded in the black ghettos of twenty-three U.S. cities. With respect to the loss of lives and property damage, the worst disorders occurred in three cities. In 1965, rioting in Los Angeles resulted in the death of thirty-four people and property damage estimated at $35 million, and 4,000 people were arrested. In 1967, Newark experienced a civil disorder during which twenty-four people were killed and property damage of $12 million resulted. Also in 1967, Detroit exploded into a major riot, resulting in the deaths of forty-three people and property damage of $32 million, and 7,200 people were arrested. The wave of civil disorders in the 1960s represented a different focus compared to race riots of an earlier period. Violence and looting during this era were directed at white-owned buildings and businesses, instead of being directed at individuals. The report of the National Advisory Commission on Civil Disorders emphasized that the disorders erupted as a result not of a single incident, but of a series of incidents connected in the minds of black residents with long-standing underlying grievances. Although specific grievances were different for each city, twelve common grievances were identified, listed below in their order of priority:

- Police practices;
- Unemployment and underemployment;
- Inadequate housing;
- Inadequate education;
- Poor recreation facilities and programs;
- Ineffectiveness of the political structure and grievance mechanisms;
- Disrespectful white attitudes;
- Discriminatory administration of justice;
- Inadequate of federal programs;
- Inadequate of municipal services;
- Discriminatory consumer and credit practices;
- Inadequate welfare programs

The Modern Era. Some historians and political scientists mark the beginning of the modern era with the passage of the Civil Rights Act of 1964, followed by the Voting Rights Act of 1965. The former act eradicated segregation and discrimination in all types of public accommodation facilities and services. The latter act removed all obstacles to becoming a registered voter. No longer were blacks required to pass literacy tests or answer difficult questions about the Constitution. The voting rolls increased by millions of new voters across the nation, particularly in the South. At the time, these two laws were thought to be the last hurdle for blacks in their historical quest for first-class U.S. citizenship. The mood of most white Americans was positive in regard to justice and equality for all Americans. Blacks were jubilant and optimistic that full citizenship appeared to be attainable. However, this was not the immediate result experienced in all states as blacks sought to exercise their rights as citizens. Many states and local jurisdictions implemented obstacles and took actions that defied federal laws. In some cases businesses refused to serve or treat black customers on an equal basis. White extremist groups expanded and continued to incite violence and intimidate the black community.

The American public at large was shocked as they watched television accounts of the blatant actions taken by white extremists and bigoted politicians in their attempts to roll back human rights laws in the South. As a result, hundreds of whites from the North joined blacks in direct protest actions designed to eliminate discrimination in accordance with federal laws. Over a period of several years, most barriers were gradually removed as a result of the organized action taken by blacks and by their white supporters and the persistence of enforcement exerted by the federal government.

The United States returned to its conservative mode in 1969 with the election of President Richard M. Nixon. From the federal perspective, a new era was beginning with a deemphasis on social programs and issues affecting minorities and other special interest groups. Jones argues that there had been an eroding commitment to bring minorities and the poor fully into the American mainstream since 1969. However, she concludes "that the changing mood can be redirected—towards realization of the promises of America".

AFRICAN-AMERICAN STEREOTYPES

One of the most pervasive problems experienced by blacks in a majority white society is that of being negatively stereotyped as a group. One's self-concept, to a large measure, is premised on the perceptions of others. Many well-intentioned white professionals view all blacks as coming from poverty and having a poor educational background. They assume blacks have low motivation and limited potential. Stereotyping is particularly damaging in the practice of education. Teachers may consciously or subconsciously have low expectations for black students and, therefore, do not use challenging and provocative teaching strategies and material. Low expectation is directly correlated with low performance. The following is a listing of twelve black stereotypes, which have persisted in the face of scientific evidence:

- ***Mental.*** Have low intellectual ability; can be trained in simple to moderate tasks.
- ***Temperament.*** Exhibit good social adaptation; are gregarious and love their community.
- ***Emotional.*** Find it easy to express emotions; have warm emotional tone and intent.
- ***Aesthetic.*** Love music and dance; have natural ability to perform.
- ***Economic.*** Show low interest in material things and money; generally lack self-reliance.
- ***Personal morals.*** Have double standards for whites and blacks; show extreme interest in sex and permissive sexual relations.
- ***Family and home life.*** Have a high common law mating rate; place mother in role of provider; have high illegitimacy rate.
- ***Religion.*** Become very emotionally involved; are inclined toward superstition and personalization of God.
- ***Law observance.*** Have a high incidence of social disorder; engage in fighting and public drunkenness.
- ***Public manners.*** Are loud and discourteous; are careless in speech and dress.
- ***Racial pride.*** Reach only a low level of development; have inferiority feelings; accept white standards of beauty.
- ***Racial unity.*** Lack cohesion; have a high rate of intragroup conflict; distrust leadership.

These black stereotypes emerged during the 1950s. Some of them may have dissipated or changed over time. However, a national poll conducted by the University of Chicago in 1990 shows that despite progress in race relations since the 1950s, whites' negative images of blacks and other minorities continue to be pervasive. Table 9.1 provides a breakdown of white perceptions of five behavioural and personality characteristics of two minority groups. These beliefs about minorities partially explain white resistance to government assistance and affirmative action. The poll results are significant in all five categories white respondents in more than 50 percent of the sample held negative perceptions of minorities.

Table 9.1. Percentage of White Stereotyping: Two Minority Groups, 1990

	Prefer To Live Off Welfare	Likely To Be Lazy	Violence Prone	Less Intelligent	Less Patriotic
African Americans	78	62	56	53	51
Hispanic Americans	74	56	50	55	61

HISTORICALLY RELATED EDUCATIONAL ISSUES

Education has always been a highly valued goal in the African-American community. Franklin points out in his study that the black community regarded education and self-determination as prerequisites for freedom. Before the 1950s a major segment of the specialized educational programs for adults was provided by social and cultural organizations. These efforts concentrated on literacy work and job training. Along with government-initiated programs and generally expanded educational opportunities, black social groups continued to provide adult education to target populations mostly in the urban centers. Many novel arrangements were observed during this period. Black private groups had acquired the basic infrastructure (e.g., buildings, equipment, and transportation), which led to the development of partnerships with public schools and black colleges. Franklin emphasizes that the response from the black community to provide adult education "reflected the core values of black 'self-determination' and 'education' that were deeply embedded in African-American culture and experiences". This brief descriptive account is typical of many historical efforts to focus on group self-improvement through education. It therefore can be established that there is a culturally associated value system that has high regard for the traditions of education and self-help.

Adult education and community development concepts are compatible with these historic features. However, cultural and political considerations are key elements in the black self-determination process. They are likely to be sensitive and misinterpreted by those professional adult educators who lack sufficient knowledge and understanding of the historic aspects of the black experience.

MEXICAN-AMERICANS

The Spanish occupation of what is now the south-western United States predates the establishment of the American union. This area was a Spanish colony until Mexico gained its independence in 1821. In 1538, the Mexicans had assembled a printing press in Mexico City, which supported the literacy work of a university established in 1551. This historical fact suggests that Mexicans were engaged in adult education long before any other people in North America. The Spanish colony that Mexico inherited included the present area of Mexico and the vast territory north of the Rio Grande River (i.e., Texas, Arizona, New Mexico, Nevada, Colorado, and California).

It was not until the nineteenth century that any large number of white settlers from the central and eastern U.S. states and colonies set up residence in the territory under

Mexican sovereignty. In fact, the Mexican government offered grants to white settlers to farm and graze the land. At this time, there were about 18,000 settlers in what is now Texas. The policy of the Mexican government was to encourage more Anglos (English-speaking whites) to settle in the Southwest. Mexican farmers and horsemen taught the Anglos how to survive in the desert, irrigate and cultivate land, raise cattle, and breed horses.

However, this encouragement and assistance increasingly proved not to be in the best interest of the Mexican government. As the Anglo settler population grew, so did serious problems between the U.S. and Mexican governments. In 1835, the Mexican constitution was amended to eliminate many local land rights. Some Mexicans and all Anglo settlers revolted, declaring Texas a U.S. state in 1845. Mexico declared war, and a U.S. victory was concluded in 1847 with the occupation of Mexico City. Except for the territory acquired through the Gadsden Purchase of 1853, all Mexican land north of the Rio Grande was ceded to the United States.

Mexican citizens living in the territory were given the opportunity to return to Mexico without penalty or to remain and become U.S. citizens after one year of residence. Property rights would be respected and protected during the one-year period. A majority of Mexicans in the territory decided to become American citizens, even though the Mexican government had offered them resettlement assistance and land grants. According to Guerra, increasing political instability in Mexico was the main reason most of them decided to stay.

At this time, the majority of people living in the southwestern territory were Mexican-Americans. However, this was soon to change with the growth of cotton and cattle farms in Texas and the discovery of gold in California. Anglos poured in from the East in such magnitude as to outnumber Mexican-Americans living in the territory. This influx brought about greater hostility between Anglos and Mexican-

Americans, particularly in Texas. The entire area between the Nueces and Rio Grande rivers was the scene of lawlessness and rioting. Increasing numbers of black slaves were being imported to the area, which negatively influenced Anglo attitudes relative to racially mixed Mexican-Americans. Although Mexican-Americans were not considered as subhumans, as in the case of blacks, they were generally perceived to be racially inferior to Anglo-Americans.

In California, businesses and legal systems based on Anglo-Saxon principles were perceived to be a threat and foreign to the traditional Spanish model. Mexican-Americans with old land titles found it difficult to validate them through the new legal order. This was particularly true because the U.S. system of land taxation was based on the assessed value of the land. The Spanish system taxed the value of the commodity that was produced on the land. Because of the new method of land taxation, many Mexican-Americans were forced to give up land held in families for centuries. Many of these lands were sold at public tax auctions for as little as twenty-five cents per acre. With the decline of economic affluence came a corresponding decline in political influence that impacted these Mexican-American families who had acquired enormous wealth and power.

The period following the Mexican Revolution witnessed the immigration of some 75,000 Mexicans to the southwestern United States. This mass exodus of Mexican immigrants came about principally because of the economic collapse and political instability in Mexico. This was a period of economic expansion in the United States, with the rise of cotton cultivation in Texas, the growth of mining in Arizona and agriculture in Colorado, and the rapid expansion of the citrus and vegetable farms in California. These economic growth trends created an enormous demand for a large and cheap labour force for work that the Anglo population was unable or unwilling to perform. The displacement of Anglo tenant farmers in Texas by cheaper Mexican immigrants led to violence and increased hostilities. Mexican-American children were forced to attend segregated schools, and discrimination was widely practiced by Anglo businessmen and politicians alike. The Mexican Americans' response to these injustices caused them to organize and protest for change, establishing the first community organization in 1927.

Mexican-Americans suffered extreme hardship during the Great Depression of the 1930s. Many were on public relief, and some were forcibly sent back to Mexico to reduce the relief rolls. Labour unrest escalated to strikes by Mexican-American farm workers in southern California. The use of violence to break up strikes and the prohibition against the formation of unions were the prevailing means of control and suppression. Texas was the state in the Southwest where educational and health levels were the lowest. In 1943, the Mexican government refused to permit Mexican labourers to work in Texas because of discriminatory practices. By the end of World War II discrimination had been practiced against Mexican-Americans in the Southwest for over a century. This led to the formation of "barrios" in the urban centers, primarily as a result of housing discrimination. A 1962 California Welfare Commission study received testimony relative to identifying determinants and other factors responsible for the discrimination suffered by 1.5 million Mexican-Americans in California. The main points in the testimony of Juan Ramos follow:

- Early migrants did not plan to settle permanently, so they did not see the need to learn English and other American ways.
- Mexican-Americans did not trust Anglos and felt dominated by them.
- In Mexico the father was the breadwinner, but in California the mother was able to find a job much faster.

- Schools serving the barrio were inferior and caused many Mexican youth to drop out.
- Mexican men could only find hard, manual labor-type jobs.
- Many Mexican-American women were unable to obtain social services because with their limited English they could not explain their problems.

CHICANO CIVIL RIGHTS MOVEMENT

The period following the end of World War II marks the era in which Mexican-Americans initiated organizational strategies designed to secure "basic" civil rights through increased political awareness and levels of participation. When Mexican-American veterans returned to their homes after the Korean War, the gap between what they were exposed to in the military and what they found upon their return was astounding. These returning veterans increased the struggle to deal with many kinds of discrimination. Gradually voter registration and participation increased through the organized efforts of such groups as the Political Association of Spanish Organizations (PASO) in Texas and the Mexican-American Veterans Organization in Texas, California, and New Mexico. These organizations and many others have been very successful in promoting the candidacy of Mexican-American politicians. During the 1960s the basic civil rights movement of Mexican-Americans merged into the coalition of national civil rights organizations, which supported the passage of the Civil Rights Act of 1964.

An emerging cultural component of the Chicano civil rights movement is the ongoing redefinition and rediscovery of traditional Mexican culture and values. Two important focal points in this movement involve the rejuvenation of the spirit of *La Raza* and *familia*. *La Raza* centers on the belief that all "Mexican-Americans are united by a common spiritual bond and have a responsibility to help each other". Familia refers to the significant development of interpersonal relationships based on the extended family concept. Traditional Mexican culture stresses that the extended family is a source of security where individuals play specific roles so as to strengthen the family as a humanistic institution. Biculturalism as a goal requires that majority Americans recognize that Mexican-Americans can function effectively in U.S. society at the same time they are maintaining their cultural heritage. Biculturalism is antithetical to the melting-pot theory. According to **Ramirez**, *educational policies based on the melting-pot theory cause a breakdown in family relations among those Mexican-American youths who identify exclusively with Anglo-American values*. The melting-pot theory also prevents the development of bicultural identity, which expands the world view of the individual and promotes satisfying relations in two cultural worlds.

STEREOTYPES OF MEXICAN-AMERICANS

Actual knowledge and sensitivity of many majority Americans regarding the cultural characteristics of Mexican-Americans represent stereotypes that can cause a serious breakdown in interpersonal relations. Many of these judgments (stereotypes) are considered innate in the culture, affecting all but a small fraction of Mexican-Americans. While there are countless stereotypes about Mexican-Americans, the following nine statements represent some of the most prevalent:

1. *Machismo* is viewed as a negative characteristic of male behaviour. This involves excessive drinking, fighting, cursing, etc. The male is considered to be superior to the female. The man completely dominates his wife and ignores his children. There is a low regard for education and a belief in the need for children to begin working at a certain age.
2. *Resistant to change* from traditional Mexican customs and behaviours, they prefer the old ways as a guide to living.

3. They are *unfriendly* to non-Mexican strangers and do not initiate interaction.
4. Having a *fatalistic* view of the world, they feel they have no control over nature, government, and community institutions.
5. They are *nonjoiners* of voluntary community associations, including church-related and civic associations.
6. Children receive *severe punishment*, with the use of a great deal of physical force.
7. *Immediate gratification* and a failure to plan for the future are typical; they have no long-term goals.
8. They *refuse to speak English*; even though most have the proficiency, they pretend they have low-level skills or are unable to speak the language.
9. They are *intellectually inferior*, generally, to the Anglo-American.

Most Mexican-Americans are aware of the foregoing stereotypes, which are harboured by a substantial number of Anglo-Americans. These unfounded beliefs result in institutional discriminatory practices against Mexican-Americans in employment, housing, social services, and educational opportunities.

HISTORICALLY RELATED EDUCATIONAL ISSUES

The past and present social environments present a direct challenge to adult education. The scope of the psychosocial, political, and educational problems of this minority group demands interactions that reflect specific needs that are widespread as a result of generations of neglect and mistrust.

Throughout the 1950s and 1960s a great amount of time was spent by educators and community activists in programs concerned with learning to speak English and qualifying for citizenship and voter registration. While a great deal has been accomplished, much more is needed to enhance the survivability of Mexican-Americans and their communities. The discriminations suffered by the majority of Mexican-Americans in the Southwest were due to a lack of power to compel the larger community to listen and to accommodate their needs and interests. New designs of community development are needed to build on the successes of the past into the next century. Young Chicanos, bicultural in their outlook, will be planning strategies that emphasize "cultural democracy" in their quest for political and economic parity for the Mexican-American community.

NATIVE AMERICANS

Indians are the descendants of wandering nomads from Asia. It is estimated that they came to America from Asia about 20,000 years ago by crossing the Bering Strait over ice and over land bridges. A research finding in 1990 indicates that nearly 95 percent of American Indians are descendants of a single small migratory group. Studies of gene structures enable researchers to trace maternal ancestry. Douglas Wallace, a geneticist, reports that the "analysis of mitochondrial DNA from American Indians showed that the vast majority descended from four women in that original migratory group".

Many successive waves of migrants came and slowly spread all over America. Each group claimed its own land for hunting and farming. When Columbus came to the New World, there were over 350 Indian tribes in North America. Each had its own language and customs and occupied its own territory.

The arrival of white men in the New World in the Fifteenth century brought about many changes in Indian life. Waves of explorers and colonizers swept over the continent in search of gold and other rich minerals. In the process, many Indian rights were violated, which created tensions and conflicts. White men also brought with them new diseases, such as measles, smallpox, tuberculosis, influenza, and gonorrhea, which caused epidemics that killed thousands of Indians.

There were about 1 million Indians in North America when the white men came. Most white settlers who came to America wanted Indian lands. They usually tried to take the land by persuasion and, at the same time, to make the Indians move away. The British and Americans made hundred of treaties with the Indians and paid for thousands of acres in cash and material goods. But the Indians did not fully understand the colonists' ways of land transactions. For example, when Indians signed a treaty, they thought they had sold rights to use the land, not rights to *own* the land itself. Through other devious methods, white men often cheated the Indians and broke most of the treaties. They regarded Indians as savages without souls and felt that they could treat the Indians like wild beasts. As white settlers pushed westward, disrupting Indian life and settling on Indian lands, many massacres and wars resulted. The first Indian assault on settlers occurred in Jamestown, Virginia, in 1622. Ironically, this town was also the port of entry for the first African slaves in 1619. Indian wars lasted almost 280 years, and the Indian population was reduced from I million plus in 1620 to about 400,000 in 1900.

The United States started organizing reservations for Indians in 1786. In 1830, Congress passed the Indian Removal Act, which gave the government the authority to move all Indians westward beyond the Mississippi River to make room for thousands of new white settlers. The vast territory designated for relocation was considered to be a "desert." But in a few years, whites also began settling in this territory, causing Indians to be forced onto smaller reservations.

Today, Indians are not forced to live on reservations, but most of them do because the land is tax-free and because they desire to preserve remnants of traditional Indian culture. The United States has about 100 reservations, which are managed by the Bureau of Indian Affairs. Canada has about 2,200 Indian reserves, managed by the Indian Affairs Branch. Both governments provide free education and medical services for Indians on reservations. Life on the reservation has caused the American Indian to lose many cultural values and customs. In the past, "tribal groups were forbidden to practice their religion, ceremonial dancing, language, and other valued cultural activities". Over the years, the U.S. government's goal has been to assimilate Indians into the larger society. Reservation Indians have generally resisted government efforts for assimilation.

ACCULTURATION OF INDIANS

Historically, Indians have rejected government efforts to assimilate them into the larger American society. Even some Indians who tried to understand and promote ethnic assimilation could not understand the emphasis of educational and cultural programs that glorified Europe while at the same time de-emphasizing Indian cultural values and beliefs.

According to **Tjerandsen**, *effective assimilation of a large number of people from a culturally different population requires that a process referred to as acculturation be encouraged and allowed to develop as a precursor to assimilation.* Tjerandsen defines acculturation as "the process by which the culture of a society that is in prolonged touch with another society subsequently changes". Apparently government policymakers and administrators failed to understand this prerequisite as a requirement for the integration of a people into a larger society. Acculturation starts with individuals and groups of a target population, rather than with policy and program conceptualizations, which ultimately lead to legislation and regulations. Where these laws governing Indian affairs failed, the typical response of the government was to amend the law or create a new law without collaboration with a cross-section of Indian leaders, and with very little understanding of Indian culture, values, and customs.

Table 9.2 provides a juxtaposed listing of some Anglo-American values and Indian values. Without question, there are serious and deep conflicts, which must be modified in the process of acculturation. Accommodations must be made on both sides in an effort to achieve bicultural cooperation, trust, and respect.

Table 9.2. Conflicts in Cultural Values

Anglo-American Middle-Class Values	Navajo Indian Traditional Values
1. Mastery over nature to control subjugate, and overcome	1. Harmony with nature in maintaining the state.
2. Scheduled living.	2. Non-scheduled living.
3. Future-oriented.	3. Present-oriented.
4. Competitive individualism.	4. Non-competitive deference to group needs.
5. Acceptance of others on the basis of roles and status.	5. Acceptance of others on the basis of demonstrated integrity.
6. Punishment is related to guilt.	6. Punishment is related to shame.
7. Representative democracy.	7. Face-to-face government, minimum tribal leadership.
8. Individuality, fame and recognition emphasized.	8. Anonymity and humility stressed.
9. Cultural aspiration to achieve at a higher level than parents.	9. Cultural aspiration to follow in the ways of elders.
10. Save for the future.	10. Share resources and wealth with those who need it today.

This difficult undertaking must be approached from an evolutionary perspective, which requires changes and/or mutual regard for cultural attitudes, habits, intrinsic values, and world view. If any meaningful acculturation is to occur, those essential elements of Indian heritage that provide the central group identity as it relates to survival and growth in coping with the larger society must be safeguarded.

Oversimplification and generalization about Indians and their culture will continue to be provocative sources of research for many years to come. There is a critical lack of knowledge about *aboriginal* Indian culture, which will help in understanding the reservation culture of today. There must be a greater *involvement* of Indians themselves concerning research and programming efforts. Indians must be in the vanguard of making choices and developing solutions in a way that is compatible with life styles, customs, and the need for self-determination.

HISTORICALLY RELATED EDUCATIONAL ISSUES

Indian cultures have been stressed to the point of transformative dimensions brought about through the reservation culture. However, it must be recognized that Indians are a diverse group, found at all levels of the acculturation continuum. In spite of this diversity, Regan and Pagano contend that there is a generally accepted set of social values, which are found in varying degrees in all Indian groups. The writers further charge that adult basic education has failed because texts and other written instructional materials do not reflect Indian culture and often contradict its values and taboos. Most adult education efforts reported by Kersey and French had poor or minimal results. From this history, it can be properly presumed that traditional methods operating on Western Anglo assumptions are likely to fail.

Indian activists found in urban centers in the 1960s, discovered that there was power in organizing. In 1975, the U.S. Congress committed itself to a policy of "self-determination" by providing maximum Indian participation in the government and education of Indian people". Indians have consistently resisted assimilation and integration to a large extent. They have continued to protest and agitate for self-determination. Adult education and community development from the Indian perspective can be utilized to accelerate the social change that they seek. Adult education professionals have an opportunity to learn, share, and assist in the development of culturally distinct independent communities. In this development, adult education can play an important role in efforts to prepare people for jobs, effective health care, functioning economies, and good schools.

COMMON SOCIOECONOMIC FACTORS

Despite the diversity and complexity of each minority group, there are three broad categories of socio-economic factors that affect all minorities in varying degrees. They are *poverty*, *educational attainment*, and *employment discrimination*. A limited critique of these socio-economic factors is provided.

POVERTY

The persistence of poverty in an affluent United States is a perplexing historic phenomenon. Some citizens through their herculean efforts are able to escape poverty status as a permanent lifestyle. Generally, the 1990 poverty level is estimated and defined as a total family (four members) with an annual income of $10,000 or less. By this definition, in 1987, 29.9 percent of black families and 26 percent of Hispanic families lived below the poverty level.

Despite massive government assistance of the past, coupled with present efforts, a central core of individuals and families seems to be destined to live in poverty year in and year out. This segment of impoverished citizens is sometimes referred to as the underclass. This term may have negative connotations for some analysts who suggest that it implies a pathological cycle, which cannot be reversed in the normal scheme of life. A large proportion of the

American *underclass* is minorities. Most live in the central cities, with a growing component emerging in nearby suburban communities. In studying the underclass, Sawhill identified 880 underclass neighbourhoods, which appeared to have four common characteristics: (1) many high school dropouts, (2) many unemployed, (3) welfare recipients, and (4) single-female-headed households. Fifty-nine percent of the residents were black, and 12 percent were Hispanic. She estimated that about 5 percent of African-Americans live in underclass areas.

EDUCATIONAL ATTAINMENT

Although there has been a marked increase in the high school completion rates of all minorities, this has not resulted in closing the gap between minorities and their white counterparts. This may be explained partially by the fact that educational attainment has expanded for all segments of U.S. society. In 1980, the high school completion rate for white adults twenty-five years and older was 70.5 percent, compared with 51.2 percent for blacks and 45.3 percent for Hispanics. Compared with younger cohorts aged seventeen to eighteen, the high school completion rate for whites was 83 percent, blacks 72 percent, Chicanos 55 percent, and Indians 55 percent. In 1985, Hispanics increased their high school graduation rate to 62.5 percent, and blacks to 75.6 percent. The Hispanic population grew by 39 percent in 1989, but their high school completion rate declined to 56 percent; for blacks it was 76.1 percent.

Illiteracy can often be determined by examining high school completion rates. However, this may be seriously misleading. In recent years there have been thousands of documented cases in which high school graduates could not read at functional levels. Kozol points out that 44 percent of black adults read at very low levels. For those minorities for whom English is not the mother tongue (including Mexican-Americans and Indians), alarming rates of illiteracy and low levels of educational attainment have occurred. Roughly 45 percent of urban Indians and less than 35 percent of Indians who live on reservations have completed high school. Data on school dropouts have consistently shown that Mexican-American youth have the highest dropout rates and leave school earlier than the other groups.

Although blacks and other minorities have made gains over the past decades, there is still a long way to go to achieve parity. Most analytic studies show a high correlation between educational attainment and good employment. In 1985, nearly 28 percent of Hispanic youth and more than 15 percent of black youth ages sixteen to twenty-five dropped out of high school.

EMPLOYMENT DISCRIMINATION

Racial discrimination continues to be a major problem in the lives of minorities. The Urban Institute conducted a study to measure treatment given black and white men interviewing for entry-level jobs. The study used pairs of specially trained black and white male college students who were matched in all important characteristics age, education, work experience, physical build, and speech. The study teams responded to job advertisements in Washington, D.C., and Chicago. The study confirmed that blacks and whites received unequal treatment by employers. Whites were offered jobs 20 percent of the time, compared with 7 percent of the time for blacks. The findings of this 1991 study "suggest a pervasive pattern of discrimination in America's urban labour markets and argue for a strong program of auditing and enforcement of equal opportunity laws". A 1989 Urban Institute study measuring treatment of Hispanic and white applicants found that Hispanics were subjected to a higher degree of discrimination than blacks. "In 31 percent of the white Hispanic audits, the white candidate received more favourable treatment".

Black unemployment for males is twice that for white males, and Hispanic unemployment is 20 percent higher than white unemployment. The same comparative data on education attainment discussed earlier in this chapter emphasize the gap at all levels between whites and minorities. These historic and continuing discrepancies have serious negative implications for employment opportunities in the near future. In an analysis of job changes expected between now and the year 2000, it is projected that low-skill jobs will be declining and that jobs requiring higher levels of skills and education will be on the increase.

In addition to the preceding three broad socio-economic factors briefly discussed, the Business-Higher Education Forum's report *Three Realities* identifies four common elements that affect minorities in all groups. These pervasive elements are historic and remain as contextual impediments to the progress of minority life in the United States. They are : (1) racism, (2) the quality of available education, (3) the stranglehold of the inner city, and (4) the lack of participation in all aspects of the nation's economic life.

FUTURE DIRECTIONS

Each of the preceding discussions of the three minority groups provides a historical and socio psychological perspective that has serious implications for the educational needs of each group. The needs must be considered in the context of past treatments and responses to ameliorate long-standing oppression and discrimination by the larger society. Each group must be examined separately because of its unique root problem in the larger society and the different evolutionary conditions and circumstances that have brought it to the present juncture.

Some problems and issues can be generalized to all minorities. But each has its own historical and psychosocial functions, which have served to shape and mold its current status and relationship with the dominant group in U.S. society. Ancestors of Indians and Mexican-Americans were on the soil long before Columbus made his voyage to the New World. Blacks were captured in Africa and brought forcibly to the Americas as slaves. During a 300-year period, all three groups were subjected to extremely oppressive measures the seeming permanence of slavery, war and isolation on reservations, and the loss of territory and entrepreneurship.

These histories, with their recurring themes of conservative, moderate, and radical movements, have conditioned minorities to constantly adjust and readjust to the prevailing moods of the dominant culture. Consequently, minorities have been reactive rather than proactive to the dynamics of U.S. society. Generally, each group has rejected the melting-pot theory and as a result has not benefited from public education, which historically has offered a monocultural curriculum model rather than one that recognizes cultural pluralism.

There has been ample attention in the literature to the need for multicultural approaches to educating minority youth and adults. However, there has not been significant reform from public education systems on a national scale. Community-based programs have experienced success in implementing multicultural approaches because their basic survival depends on the voluntary attendance of adult learners in the community. To some extent, public education can learn much from community-based programs. Greater research is needed to describe and analyze the diversity of community-based education, particularly as it is effective in serving minority populations.

The challenge to serve minority populations must reflect knowledge of their histories, psychosocial patterns, and socio-economic needs. Potential learners should be involved in the design and evaluation of programs offered for community improvement. Cultural pluralism as an operational curriculum concept will undoubtedly plague public educational programs for many years to come. Therefore, the nonformal community-based strategy has the flexibility to offer immediate benefits to segments of minority populations who have been otherwise poorly served or isolated by public education.

SUMMARY

In this chapter a rationale was offered relative to the necessity of focusing on those segments of the population that have not benefited from the formal educational system commensurate with the majority population. Consequently, minorities find themselves at the bottom rung of the socio-economic ladder. Three identifiable cultural minority groups were discussed: African-Americans, Mexican-Americans, and Native Americans.

The educational problems of minority Americans are deeply intertwined with their unique histories of isolation and discrimination. Current issues cannot be properly interpreted without some insight into historical antecedents. A brief historical narrative was provided for each minority group, including a discussion of different values and beliefs espoused by each group. To the extent possible, a relationship between those values and education was mentioned. All groups are negatively impacted by certain stereotypes, which persist in the United States in spite of the general expansion of education and the affluence of the majority population.

The challenges to adult education and community development from the formal perspective are twofold. The first is to foster a resurgence of institutional efforts to initiate equal-level innovative partnerships in minority communities. The second, is to develop multicultural educational support systems that reflect the learning styles, motivations, and aspirations of adult learners in the autonomous capacity building of community leadership.

Given the uniqueness of each group, it was stressed that they all suffer disproportionately from three common maladies: poverty, illiteracy, and employment discrimination. Finding remedies and the political will to significantly ameliorate these maladies undoubtedly has implications for the national economic, political, and social well-being of the society as it faces a dynamic technological era.

❑❑❑

10

Planning in a Community-based Adult Education

INTRODUCTION

Community-based program planning attempts to address the needs of both individuals and the community at large and can be undertaken in various forms ranging from determination by "experts," with little community involvement in the process, to determination by communities themselves. Unfortunately, much of the program planning that occurs within community-based situations relies on "expert" advice and is required to follow prescriptive models. This denies the community opportunities to grow and develop. Models that emphasize step-by-step procedures in program planning focus on the outcomes or content of program planning. This approach produces programming but often fails to promote community. Recent theorizing in program planning, however, stems from the critical perspective that attempts to build community through democratic processes while examining contextual factors and power relationships.

Significant education occurs in the process of planning and implementing programs, particularly through dialogue and community building that is inherent in community-based organizations. In turn, the degree of learning is affected by both the interests that each participant brings to the situation and the power relationships that exist in the situation itself. How these two contextual factors, interests and power relationships, are negotiated is key to the realization of community programs.

The move in recent years toward standardization and efficiency in programming reveals societal trends that are more concerned with the bottom line than with learner development. This occurs throughout the educational process, as students have less control over their education. Appropriate process is sacrificed for product. The planning of educational programs is affected in that programs are prescribed, determined by someone other than the learner. The concern is primarily outcome based focusing on specific skill development. It is difficult for students to own the process of education when it is irrelevant and insensitive to the needs of the learner. Fortunately, there are still pockets where a more holistic notion of education is practiced. The case study presented here examines the program planning process in an organization, Candora, that serves women who have been marginalized for various reasons. The planning process provides the women with a means of becoming empowered within their own lives as well as within their communities. The question that guided us as we entered Candora was to what extent do power relationships affect the program planning process in a fundamentally democratically conceived community-based organization?

Sork and Caffarella analysed program planning theories and models from the last 40 years and determined six elements were common to all of them: (a) scan the environment, (b) run a needs assessment, (c) develop an administrative plan, (d) develop an instructional plan, (e) implement the program, and (f) evaluate the program. They also admitted, however, that little is known about how planners deal with contextual factors. Cervero and Wilson investigated the "political richness, ethical dilemmas, and practical judgments of planning practice" in institutional settings. They concluded that each planning situation is affected by the *interests* that each party brings to the exercise, the *power relationships* that exist within it, and how the program planner *negotiates* these interests and power relationships in developing the program. They suggested the planner should be promoting a democratic ethos in the planning situation. Drawing upon Forester (1989), they developed four strategies that planners could use depending on the boundaries or limits that exist for various situations. They referred to their model as bounded rationality in program planning.

The case study that follows uses this theoretical framework, but it extends Cervero and Wilson's work into a community-based context. In such settings, community programmers usually use a community development planning model; however, that model does not explain how negotiation occurs in collectivity, nor does it highlight the dilemmas the planners encounter when attempting to practice democracy in community. The research reported here addresses these problems. Specifically, it seeks to illuminate processes that are important in overcoming the fragmentation of contemporary society: relationship building, critiquing power structures, and acting in concert on shared goals.

The community-based organization selected for this case study is different from other groups with similar purposes in its orientation to planning and in the functioning of the organization. As a women's collective, Candora serves low-income women who come together to overcome problems of poverty, family violence, child care, unemployment, language barriers, and settlement issues. They operate on a consensual basis, and programs are developed based on the needs and interests of these women.

The following involves both descriptive and theoretical analyses drawn from the data and the literature. A discussion then illustrates the ways they fit with the bounded rationality model of Cervero and Wilson and ties the findings back to critical social theory.

CANDORA

Candora is a nonprofit organization that was originally established as part of the consumer education project of Grant MacEwan Community College in Edmonton, Alberta. It grew out of the Abbotsfield Women's Project, which came into being through a participatory education approach. This approach was new to the consumer education project because it had previously followed an "expert" approach to program planning. Candora continues to operate on a participatory model in which community members determine their own future.

The mission statement of Candora involves a series of principles as follows:

They, of the CANDORA Society of Edmonton, are people working together to effect change in their lives and their community.

1. They honour the strengths and capabilities that we have;
2. They are the experts on our life experiences;
3. They have the potential for change and growth;
4. They maintain the control of our lives;
5. They participate in education for personal and social change;
6. They employ skilled people;
7. They strive to create a cohesive and mutually supportive atmosphere for all who live our neighborhood.

The residents of Abbotsfield and Rundle areas determine the programs that are offered; a coordinator is hired by the board. Many residents are hired to work as community facilitators. The participatory approach is helped along through the interests of the first coordinator, as well as women in the community who have had experience in this type of grassroots community development in their native Latin American countries.

Candora stands for Can Do in Rundle and Abbotsfield, which are areas of the city of Edmonton located in the northeast quadrant. These two areas were built in the 1970s during the boom years in Alberta and were intended for low income housing. Although the city originally provided funding for the housing complexes, this eventually ceased with dwindling municipal budgets. Eventually, the decreased value of the declining housing made them affordable to those on social assistance and to the working poor.

Single-parent families, primarily headed by women, make up a large portion of the population of the communities. Many of the women who live in the area are isolated, without family or friends, and operate in the private sphere rather than in the public sphere. Candora provides a space for these people to come together, to meet people, and to identify and to take action on some of the problems they are experiencing, such as unemployment, poverty, family violence, parenting, and child-care concerns. The community is also home to a diverse group of immigrants, and Candora provides them with a place to address their language and settlement concerns in a collective manner. Other programs in Candora include native crafts, sewing, cooking, parenting, a Spanish support group, and collective kitchens.

The organization is based in the local Abbotsfield Mall and is open 4 days per week. The programs and staff are funded through Alberta Social Services, City of Edmonton Community Support Services, and various private foundations. The staff consists of a coordinator, the Building A Business Towards Self-Employment program coordinator, three outreach workers, an administrative/financial coordinator, and a child-care worker. Programs include the Personal and Community Enrichment Program (PACE), which provides most of the base funding, and are designed to give those who have been out of the workforce for a long time a preliminary introduction to the workplace. Residents participate in a Tuesday morning weekly "life choices" program (part of the PACE program) and are paid 5 hours per week for work in Candora. It is in this group where programs are planned, where women give voice to issues, and where a constant renaming of who they are takes place. Programs are initiated and implemented in the life choices group; it is here that the knowledge the women possess is exercised, taken seriously, brought to fruition, and realized. Women who participate in this program learn they have potential and a contribution to make to society. They learn to cope with their difficulties, and they learn to be confident so they can step out of poverty and take an active role in society. In affirming the success of the project, one official in social services said, "Candora is *where* we all need to be."

VOICES AT CANDORA

To determine how program planning occurs in Candora, both a group interview and individual interviews were held in the summer of 1994. The group interview, comprising about 20 people, was conducted during the Tuesday morning life choices program. At a later date three staff members and one resident were interviewed.

The information that came out of the interviews was analyzed according to: (a) the various stakeholder interests (the women, the staff, the founders), (b) the power relationships within and outside of Candora that affect the way programs are planned, and (c) how these interests and power relationships are negotiated in the program-planning process. We present the themes unique to Candora within the framework of their interests, power relationships, and negotiations and highlight the ways Candora women practice program planning.

INTERESTS

Cervero and Wilson quoted Morgan in defining interests as "predispositions embracing goals, values, desires, expectations and other orientations and inclinations that lead a person to act in one direction or another". Each stakeholder brings his or her own interests to the program-planning situation. With Candora, these are the women, staff, and external groups whose interests must be given consideration.

WOMEN OF CANDORA

The women who participate in Candora have interests ranging from personal self-interests to public self-interests. Specifically, the personal self-interests include the need to connect with others to talk about personal crises or to overcome loneliness. The need to connect with others is an undertone in the following statement by a resident: "I didn't know what to do or where to go, and I was really new to this community.

When Candora began I came here, and after some months I know the necessity to help in this neighbourhood because people live in poverty and I was aware of the [need in] the Spanish community.... I began to visit house by house to convince them to come here to the centre to do sewing and crafts because I understand they need to do something that they like, like sewing, crocheting, and cooking too. In this way I am here six years.

Many of the women depend on the Candora group for support and therapy when there's trouble at home. "Family violence is an issue in the Spanish community. The Centre addresses this issue." They "depend on these people [who] help many people." As another women described Candora: "This place is for everybody. It is important for me and everybody. It a place for coming and for stay three or four hours. After you go here, you go clean."

What does it mean to leave someplace "clean?" Somehow the social interaction of the group becomes a catharsis a place to get rid of the dirt. Sorting through the feelings, assumptions, and beliefs that confuse their lives in a supportive nonjudgmental group allows the women to go away clean, feeling better about themselves and knowing that others felt the same way or have moved away from immobilizing thoughts and emotions. This kind of group interaction is life giving. It affirms the self as basically good at a time when partners and society continually call them bad. As one woman put it, "Candora is my umbligo." *Umbligo* in Spanish means umbilical cord, a cord that connects a new unborn baby to a nurturing mother. Thus, metaphorically, the Candora women are being birthed and nurtured through a cord of life found in the group. Through this cord, personal interests, in time, shift from a concern for only themselves as individuals to a concern for all the women in like circumstances. They learn to address larger issues such as family violence and poverty.

The personal interests articulated in the group dialogue can be considered an emancipatory process because each woman recognized she had an interest and a need to become connected to other women. As the women congregated with others with similar problems, they gradually moved to the question, "What are *we* going to do about our situations?" Instrumental interests emerged that revolved around skills for employment. For example, one woman stated, "I got involved because I was willing to share the skills I have with the sewing department, knitting and crocheting." The women understood that their strength was in "the traditional kinds of things like cooking, cleaning and sewing. In order to be able to compete for other jobs, you need to look at a whole other area, and it seems to me that we are always doing catch up." But some are making money using their traditional skills.

I came to Candora in 1992. I was here for six months, but then was ... sick [and] did not come for one year. I went to school too. I came back in March 1994 and am volunteering again, and have another mission. I am now seeking to have a catering group, and about one month ago we took the first job, catering for about 40 people and for this Thursday, they are going to do a lunch for about 60 people for Candora's annual general meeting.

We are trying to do something like that. I was in the employment program and in the tailoring shop. I was learning to do jackets and alterations. Although economic interests are paramount to their livelihood, the women understand they need to work through their psychosocial needs as well. In time, the opportunity to share and see the larger picture in a safe and comfortable environment moved some of the women to action projects outside their own homes and outside Candora itself.

STAFF AT CANDORA

The full-time staff also express interests that are philosophically and altruistically based. They adhere to a community development model that asserts the ability of the women to define their needs and to solve their problems and issues. One of the staff's interests includes "a different way of working and a different philosophy that [attempts] to be worked out in practice. We talk a lot about honouring people and looking at strengthening capacity or working a different way but we [hardly] ever do it." In Candora, however, there is an attempt to walk the talk, to act on principles they believe in. Candora provides an opportunity to work in an egalitarian structure that honours relationships, caring, and compassion rather than hierarchies and linear thinking.

The women actively critique why they are kept poor by society in a dynamic dialogical process of naming the situation "as it is." There is an interest in working in a place that promotes "social justice and change," in a place that is congruent with personally held beliefs that social change is good and necessary for advancement of human development and quality of life:

> *So my interests were to work in a different kind of structure. I had done some workshops in popular theatre and education, some on community development; I was in the one in 1988 with John McKnight. I had harboured these thoughts that I would like to be part of this.*

The staff hoped community members would take ownership of the project. They saw their staff position as temporary and in the background, rather than in the foreground of planning or doing. The staff understood that "you plan *with* the community rather than *for* them because [planning for them] never works; nobody will ever show up. I mean that's the nature of it." Members of the community need to articulate their needs and wants from their own experiences and be able to fulfil those needs if they are to grow and develop.

The staff see a "poverty of hope amongst the women in this community." The women of the community often don't believe there's anything of value in a ghetto or run-down area. It takes a process of "naming the strengths of this community. There are a lot of wonderful things here and [recognizing] that makes people reconsider the value of this community, to stay and make those connections." The staff view their mission as drawing from "something within us that would give possibility for change." A facility is not enough; it takes personal integrity in the staff to work themselves out of a job as the community becomes more involved and committed. It's "an intent that the community finds its own potential and dynamic and they can work that through rather than my need to be there all the time. And that is really what we hope will happen."

These interests require a deep commitment on the part of staff because they believe their work is more than a "job"; it is a vocation. They have a vision with a philosophy, one that means committing to the daily life in community on a long-term basis. This prevents them from being prescriptive, rigid, or formulaic about community development, a factor that is highly important in participatory program planning. The program unfolds and becomes relational and interconnected, and the planning process itself is facilitated *with*, not "dictated" *by* the staff.

EXTERNAL GROUPS

Interests are not only generated from within Candora, but also outside of it. Funders, in particular, have interests that affect the programs that occur at Candora. In many cases, the programs that founders, particularly large bureaucracies, are willing to fund must be within their prescriptive and rigid guidelines, and they will not tolerate deviation. It is in their interest to maintain the efficiency and accountability of the programs they fund. Recent policy changes that focus on the number of people that can be "put through" programs in the least amount of feasible time fits with the conservative philosophy and interest of the present government. Because the funders' interests do not always match Candora's interests, conflicts and tensions about programming develop.

The one thing that is becoming increasingly apparent to me is that the way we operate already has come in conflict with the expectations of funders because we try to be responsive, fluid, flexible, yet we are hearing strategic planning, long-term goals, accountability and those things may or may not be compatible. It puts us in some kind of jeopardy because how can we honour the strengths here and be responsive to the women and children and what is important in the area if we are being dictated to by people who say that you will use your money in a certain way.

Other external groups often request input by Candora on proposed programs. In many instances these organizations or individuals have not really talked to the residents of the community to any large extent, and their programs or suggestions are prescriptive. The women of Candora articulate their opinions and thoughts on these issues or programs, and in general these outside interests do not seem to have much influence on the programs that are developed at Candora. It is apparent that the programs that are successful in the Candora area are conceived, initiated, and implemented by the Candora women themselves.

POWER RELATIONSHIPS

Cervero and Wilson suggested that power relationships exist in all human interactions and it is a vital part of the relationship among people in the program planning process. They quote Isaac in defining power as “the capacity to act, distributed to people by virtue of the enduring social relationships in which they participate”. Essentially, power relationships define what people are able to do and say.

Power relationships occur both from outside of the group, as well as within. The major external power relationships occur with the funders. Because of Candora’s philosophy of “people before programs,” the organization has a bottom line that they are not willing to step over in compromising their principles for the sake of funding. The most classic example that jeopardized Candora’s future is a funding proposal for a long term existing program. The guidelines for this program had changed, and the funding agency required that the same program be completed in a much shorter period of time. The funder was a government agency and the approach was consistent with policy from a new government pushing for standardization and efficiency. The staff at Candora knew that they needed a longer period of time to accomplish what was best for the participants. They stood firm, presented their arguments, were not willing to become an extension of the state, but ultimately the funding for the program was revoked. This base funding has not been fully replaced, and as time goes on the ability to continue to fund programs and staff becomes increasingly difficult for the organization. The power of the dominant system continues to threaten Candora’s survival.

Although power relationships are easier to identify outside an organization, internal organizational power relationships exist. Candora considers itself a flat organization structurally; however, the existence of a paid professional who acts as coordinator implies some hierarchy. She described her position:

> *The staff attempts to ground me, but I am in a different position, and even though we work in an organization where everyone's input is important and so on, there is still some levelling that is bound to be the case because you are the boss so you have to take that role on at certain times more than others.*

Staff members have certain authority over their respective areas, but they make every attempt to ensure equality within the group. In terms of program planning, although staff may introduce an idea for a program that they feel is appropriate, the decision is still up to the women, who may or may not go along with these ideas. Still, the staff have power in that they decide on what type of funding to apply for or what issues to bring to the group. Certainly, there is leadership here and staff must be aware of their motives.

Power relationships that emerge and cause conflicts within the group are handled through dialogue with the group as a whole. Power relationships within the organization can be fragmenting, and the group attempts to prevent this from occurring through a culture of respect and tolerance for everyone.

NEGOTIATION

Cervero and Wilson suggested that negotiation is the main activity planners undertake in developing programs. It allows them to connect and balance the interests and power relationships that exist in the planning situation. Planners negotiate their interests *with* others, as well as negotiate *between* other interests and power relationships. As this occurs, they negotiate *about* the interests and power relationships that structure the situation. Planners then can act *within* the social context and act *upon* it through the planning process. Cervero and Wilson's research comes from institutionalized situations where the planner is charged with more direct responsibility in program planning. In participatory education, the planner becomes more of a facilitator, but ultimately must be the one to ensure that planning occurs and is implemented.

With various interests and power relationships occurring within Candora at any given time, the task of negotiating these is primarily up to the coordinator, who serves as the facilitator of program planning. Because philosophies differ, negotiations between Candora and the funders can create situations where Candora is either successful in putting their ideas across, or unsuccessful. Both situations have occurred and continue to occur:

> *I don't know that I can verbalize that, I just do it, and I don't know if I do it real well but I just do it the way it seems to work for me. I guess that if I don't like what happens at a government level and a funder level I give voice to it and try to negotiate with them so they can relax their hard line approach. And certainly [I say] written or verbally, "I don't think that you are looking at this the right way." In the end I might still have to do it and that was really true of evaluation. We gave voice really strongly and we submitted what we thought evaluation should look like and in the end it wasn't honoured and we were told "you get the funding and do it this way," and we had to live with it. I still hold the philosophy that the community needs to define for itself what has to happen.*

Negotiating between interests of participants is another part of the process. For the most part, all interests and needs are respected, although the needs of the majority are given the priority. Individual voices are provided for to the best of the collective's ability, which may mean individuals are referred to other programs or agencies that are better able to address specific needs more fully. Because of the collective nature of the group, there is a sense of equality that becomes apparent in the negotiation process:

Negotiations are on-going and there is freedom to express negative feedback without fear of reprisal of some sort. And there is the freedom, there isn't the fear of losing a job or that you are going to be alienated.

People's needs are taken into account when negotiation happens. This fits with Candora's philosophy that the people in the programs are more important than the nature of the programs themselves. This creates a different emphasis on the context and on the programs that are eventually decided on. They are not prescriptive, but rather interactive to allow for the growth and development of each individual.

FUNDAMENTAL ELEMENTS IN COMMUNITY BASED ORGANIZATIONS

Although democratic program planning is woven throughout the descriptive analysis of interests, power relationships, and negotiation outlined here, it is a secondary descriptive analysis that continues to show the uniqueness of this community-based study. Three themes were identified that have significant effects on the program-planning process in Candora. These are fundamental characteristics, we think, of community-based programming. The dominant theme is equalizing power, and the other two themes are empowerment for self-sufficiency and self-confidence, and advocating for the interests of women. They are all interconnected, but it is useful to pull them apart to illustrate the effects they have on program planning.

EQUALIZING POWER

The main theme, equalizing power, suggests power is consciously acknowledged by the staff of Candora, who attempt to level the playing field in all contexts. Thus, the staff of Candora generally see the structure of the organization as being circular or flat. This creates an ambiguous or messy situation for the coordinator who often struggles to define her role:

Equalizing power relationships to create this circular structure involves negotiating with the power relationships both inside and outside of Candora. In terms of funders, Candora's principles are made clear in all proposals, and although some funders are responsive, others are not willing to allow for any deviation from the prescriptive nature of their programs. The collective is willing to garner support from their board members, as well as local and provincial politicians, should this become necessary in ensuring their existence and in dealing with difficult funding agencies.

Equalizing power is probably more evident within the collective and its day-to-day operations than in the conflicts with outside agencies. In an effort to promote egalitarian relations and to equalize power, the coordinator told a story that illustrated what happens when visitors to Candora are not given preferential treatment.

The other thing that we used to do when we used to meet a bit more formally, like around our employment programs, we always had people coming and going. When we did introductions, ... they think that they are going to sit at the front of the room when they are going to make a presentation, and you say, "Well, just take a chair," and it is funny to watch some people. They are not sure what to do. They don't know where to sit, or should they be moving towards the front of the room. Men in particular are bad for that if they come to visit. Really they are. And when we go around the room, all of us introduce ourselves, so there really isn't anything special done. And then we might say, "and today [we have so-and-so with us] and this person is here to talk about whatever." But there is not this whole lauding given to that person that makes some sort of "stand up here above everyone else." It's trying to equalize again and give women the opportunity to feel that they have as much dignity and as much right to be sitting around that table as the big shot.

This method provides for an atmosphere where the women can sit at the same table with authority figures and feel they are on equal footing and are not "lesser people."

Even among themselves there is an acknowledgment that they are all equal. Equal time is also given to the women themselves who tell their stories in the group as funders and guests listen, often hearing for the first time their clients' voices. Despite differences in language, education, and so on, no one individual stands out above the rest. The women have come to expect that their opinions and voices will be heard, and they will call the staff on it if they feel that this is not happening. Ultimately, this feeling of collectivity provides them with a sense of power that builds their individual confidences in equalizing power in their own lives.

EMPOWERMENT FOR SELF-SUFFICIENCY AND SELF-CONFIDENCE

Through the experience of being involved in a group that promotes a culture of equalizing power when necessary, women are given the skills and confidence to undertake this kind of activity for themselves. The fact that their voices are respected within the group can be a new experience for many of them and give them the personal power to overcome some of the obstacles that have kept them in a dependent state:

> *You can put something on the table and say, "What do people think?" And some reaction can occur as opposed to saying, "Well, here it is." There is a danger for people in being honest in those kinds of cases. They probably haven't got a lot of reinforcing about that in the past. If they haven't agreed with people in positions of authority, doctors, teachers, in their past, why would they risk it? But here is hopefully a place that they can do that with us being there to say, "Feel free to disagree," and they have been.*

Respect and dignity are the key components of Candora, where people come together to help people help themselves. The notion of empowerment is inherent in everything they do. As people find power within the collective, they can overcome the lack of self-confidence that may have been holding them back from confronting the difficulties that they face. By giving voice to their opinions and being able to guide the direction of programs, their self-confidence and growing skills build their abilities to escape the cycle of dependency and to become self-sufficient. This type of empowerment, though, is not promoted from a standpoint of individualism, because it has its roots in community. Instead, it is a notion of independence through interdependence.

ADVOCATING FOR THE INTERESTS OF WOMEN

During the program-planning phase, particularly with outside agencies, the staff must continually ensure that the interests and needs of the women of Candora are communicated. Problems that these women, most of whom are single mothers living on social assistance, encounter are created by the patriarchal society in which they live. The issues they confront on a day-today basis, such as poverty and violence, are systemic; they are not an individual's problem but rather society's problem. There is an effort to assist the women in understanding they are not to blame for these problems, and various tools for doing this, such as popular theater, are used. Candora's continual voice assists in getting these issues onto the agendas for change. The education of government and agency representatives as to an alternative method of doing things, another way of looking at their "clients," promotes further understanding of what is occurring. It promotes an awareness of a reality or world view that many bureaucrats may not be willing to understand or adopt. However, advocating these interests, refusing to take a client submissive orientation, is no guarantee of change:

> *But the people in power have never been the people that share the kind of vision that John McKnight had. It is almost anti-power, so of course, the politicians and especially the civil servants are an entrenched group of people making good salaries that have no desire to see the status quo change.*

PUTTING THE THREE THEMES TOGETHER

All three of these themes are interrelated and affect the program-planning process. The type of process, as well as the type of program that eventually comes out of it, is imbued with the philosophy of the staff, particularly of the coordinator, who is the one to pull all these threads together in providing for opportunities for the women of Candora. The program planner needs to be democratic in orientation and to become aware of his or her sense of agency to deal with the structures that affect the program plan. From the research completed in this case study, it is evident that the program planner is much more openly democratic than those in the examples Cervero and Wilson provided, which were all institutionally based. It appears the grassroots nature of Candora and its non institutionalized orientation contributes to the ability of the program planner to undertake a democratic role in negotiation because of the lack of direct constraining elements on the organization. These elements appear to be more autonomous and directed from the ground up rather than top down. There is less concern about the political positioning of the coordinator, although the attempts to stand up to power brokers could have more of an overall effect on the organization than they did on the individual program planners in Cervero and Wilson's examples. For instance, in the Cervero and Wilson cases, if one of the program planners chose to advocate for a dramatic change to the *status quo*, he or she could be moved out of the job quickly. In the case of Candora, a coordinator who advocates for too dramatic a change is likely to cause funders to stop supporting the program, thus affecting himself or herself as well as the rest of the organization. Despite this, there appears to be more room for the democratically-oriented program planner to work within a community-based organization as the power comes from the grassroots.

Community education encompasses the lifelong range of learning needs, with a close integration in approach between work with children, young people and adults, and by providing educational support for community development. Its emphasis is upon the provision of community based learning and development support for individuals and groups based around identified needs and issues.

Community education was used in Scotland until 2003 to describe the combination of Adult Education, Community Development and Youth Work, which is now often referred to as Community Learning and Development. In England many Schools that were established as Community Schools have adopted a community education approach.

COMMUNITY-BASED ADULT EDUCATION

Community Based Adult Learning offers informal learning in a wide range of subjects from everyday literacy and numeracy, family learning and lipreading, to creative writing, women's groups, local history and computing.

- **CBAL** is organised into five local area teams (East, North, South, South-West, West).
- **SCLDWs:** The Senior Community Learning and Development Worker for the local area will usually have overall responsibility for literacy and numeracy provision in their area.
- **LCLDWs:** The local Community Learning and Development Worker normally organise adult literacy and numeracy groups in their area. Some have a background in adult literacy and numeracy and they usually supervise and support part time sessional group tutors.
- **Venues:** Some groups run in dedicated places, such as The Number Shop (South) and Platform (South West), others in community centres, schools, libraries or voluntary sector premises, such as Adult Learning Link (East) and Gorgie City Farm (West).

❑❑❑

11

Adult Education: Fear-Driven Models

INTRODUCTION

Publications by the business community suggest that employers *want* a more participatory (though not democratic) workplace, if only workers could contribute the right skills and attitudes. And they want to remain at their present sites rather than relocating, if only workers could get their skills "up to speed" quickly enough. Never mind that for the last 50 years workers have been actively discouraged from using most of the mental skills employers now covet, or that education programs are usually offered, maximally, 4 hours a week, with permission to attend classes often dependant on production schedules (in manufacturing) or floor coverage (in health care). This ideology primes workers to feel responsible for their own job insecurity and grateful for not being left behind.

Where unions are present to challenge this rhetoric, workers can more effectively resist the exploitative messages. When such forums don't exist, however, and workers are immersed in images of themselves as unskilled, lacking in self-esteem, and poor at communicating, workers can begin to wonder about their own abilities and potential. This self-doubt, seeded by employers' "patient" attempts to bring workers up to speed erodes the confidence needed to challenge the ideology and the status quo it protects.

One of the problems with this damaging view of worker inadequacy is that it doesn't account for the workplace as an environment that can encourage or inhibit the way workers learn and use skills. A close look at shop floors shows that workers are creative in learning and performing their jobs, resourceful in circumventing language and literacy barriers, and deliberate in their choices of when and how to use their skills. Ethnographic research has shown that workers often possess more skills than they are willing or able to demonstrate, and that many skills they do use go unrecognized by employers. Skills may go unnoticed because workers, over time, specialize in certain areas and informally divide tasks among themselves. Though each may have the knowledge needed to perform many jobs, they may have few opportunities to demonstrate that ability. Sometimes specialization (or seniority) brings workers special status that others are reluctant to challenge by showing that they, too, are skilled in a particular area. In addition, individuals develop their own strategies for approaching their work, methods that may not be recognized by managers as being equally effective ways of accomplishing their tasks. In short, workplace ethnographies raise questions about the worker deficit rhetoric by pointing out workplace constraints that prevent workers from using and expanding the skills and knowledge they already have.

The other problem is that, according to this model, the only route to "empowerment" is through individual assimilation into company values and vision of one's future. It assumes employers know what's best for workers and can be trusted to set a direction that will be healthy for company and worker alike. But we know that history doesn't bear this out, and that demonstrations of worker loyalty do not forestall downsizing, lay-offs, relocation, or the ever-increasing wage gap between workers and management. When a small manufacturing company in southeastern Massachusetts was recently bought and relocated overseas, dedicated participation in the education program did not save workers from having to work double overtime, building inventory in preparation for their own lay-offs. The new workplace is looking for employees that are willing to adapt to constant change ("lifelong learning") and accept an uncertain future.

An education program in this setting can do one of two things. It can perpetuate an ideology that defines the central problem as a workforce skills deficit, cultivating in workers a sense of indebtedness and inadequacy. Or it can support an approach of critical inquiry about work, the workplace, and the nature of the workplace education program (How does (or doesn't) the workplace function well? What knowledge and skills are valued in the workplace? What function might it serve to portray workers as the cause of economic stagnation? and so on), taking into account the competing perspectives on all of these questions.

Although necessary job-related skills can be developed through either approach, a participatory approach offers the added possibility for workers to study the messages and practices that have undermined their progress, and assert their own definition of workplace improvement. First, let's look at what the dominant model offers.

FUNCTIONAL-CONTEXT APPROACH

Most programs follow the educational model that prevails in the literature, that is, the functional context approach, which centres on teaching the immediate and localized work skills (functions) that employers feel are needed in a particular work setting (context). The specific job-related skills differ from program to program, but they are all defined primarily by the needs of the employer and the future the employer envisions for the organization. To the extent that there is union or government collaboration or both, the stakeholders identify their overlapping interests (health and safety, for instance) and leave areas where they don't agree outside the scope of the program. The shared goal of being part of (if you are the worker) or employing (if you are the employer) a more highly skilled workforce is seen as the unifying factor that supercedes labour-management differences.

In the classroom, teaching is made relevant by tying it directly to on-the job applications and daily work demands. Lessons might actively engage workers in linking what they already know to new work challenges. In this sense, the curriculum is typically student centered, drawing on worker experiences and building on strengths to develop new skills. Where there's an emphasis on practicing teamwork and problem solving, workers might also have opportunities to make suggestions about certain aspects of their own jobs. Workers generally value the chance to practice job-related skills in these traditional programs, and they appreciate the supportive encouragement they get from teachers.

When a company rewards learning by offering genuine opportunities for promotion and other incentives, these programs provide an essential service. In my experience, however, few companies have integrated their education programs into a larger human resource development effort to upgrade and promote wage workers. Fewer still have developed career or skill ladders that allow workers to take clear educational steps along a career path. (This is a strength, however, of many union-based programs.) Furthermore, because the functional context approach focuses on workers without similar attention to workplaces, it fails to consider several important factors that influence the success and credibility of a workplace program:

1. Job security does not reside in a particular set of job skills. Those that are needed today may be obsolete tomorrow, and even highly skilled workers are vulnerable to corporate trends (nurses, for example, in today's world of managed care).
2. There are risks to participating in employer-run education programs. Without a union, workers can't be sure whether to trust on-site education as an opportunity to demonstrate their commitment to learning new skills, or suspect it as a process for identifying and weeding out the undereducated. Because this is not unheard of, it's important to protect the confidentiality of student records and insure there are no repercussions for participating or not participating in a program.
3. Literacy is not inherently liberating. When the primary materials for literacy instruction are work-related texts (directions, forms, timesheets, task logs, etc.), literacy becomes a means of self-monitoring-keeping track of one's own activities for the employer rather than self-direction and autonomy.

However, people do need skills upgrading, for work and life. How can we make sure workers acquire the practical skills they need and want as we explore our understanding of the factors that shape our work futures? How do we provide opportunities to practice the skills needed to fit in as well as the skills needed to critique and transform? How can we all take responsibility for our development without accepting the myth that our access to gratifying work is completely up to us?

A PARTICIPATORY APPROACH

A participatory approach is based on the belief that the purpose of education is to expand the ability of people to become the shapers of their worlds by analyzing the social forces that have historically limited their options. As they do this, they begin to envision a new role for themselves and to identify the skills they will need to develop for this role. It incorporates both a collaborative process, which involves students in defining their own needs and negotiating the curriculum, and a content focus on understanding one's experience within a larger social context to be better prepared to act upon that context. This is not an assumption that people don't already think critically, but that making ever-new connections between our experiences and others', past and present, provides a fuller picture and clearer understanding from which to make decisions.

The participatory approach differs from a functional context approach in that it doesn't presuppose a particular solution (skills) to a predefined problem (workers). It asks participants to name the problem and cocreate an educational plan that will help them address it. And although the two often get confused, or perhaps collapsed, a participatory model also differs from a student-centered approach in that, along with an inclusive process, it focuses on critical analysis. Student-centered lessons elicit and validate student experiences and knowledge. Observations of and reflection on one's own learning is often an area of study. Participatory teaching applies this same thoughtful process to the social relations of daily life.

Consider this example. A popular student-centered lesson I know asks the class to construct a flowchart of how materials are produced at their factory. The lesson builds on the knowledge people bring, but goes beyond that to fill in gaps in their understanding—the details of certain processes or what the front office does, for example. It gives people a new perspective on how their work fits into a larger picture of the manufacturing process. This lesson often results in workers guiding others through the factory, demonstrating their expanded awareness of the work process by describing how each department should treat the next one as its customer by providing the best service possible and sharing responsibility for product quality. There's no doubt the lesson helps workers understand their surroundings and builds confidence, and it could stand alone as a successful student-centered lesson.

A participatory model would likely add a step to this, inviting workers to raise questions or comment on what they have discovered about the way the work is organized. This might lead to further investigation or to a discussion of why the work process is organized the way it is. What or whose priorities does it reflect? What are their work priorities and how would the work be designed differently for those? These activities support the discovery of what exists, but also creates space to imagine alternatives.

But is the participatory approach a realistic possibility for the workplace? Almost every workplace educator I know trying to do this kind of work describes himself or herself as "sneaking" it into the curriculum; many talk of downplaying certain lessons in their teaching reports or feeling they need to give them a different "spin." And the limited class time makes the thorough study of anything extremely difficult, especially when students have expectations of traditional coursework and hopes of measurable outcomes. Given who foots the bill for much of this education, what really are the opportunities for applying a participatory approach? I suggest that if we practice our own theory and examine the workplace as a setting that presents both barriers and possibilities, we'll discover many unexpected opportunities. Mindful of the delicate context we're working in, we can apply the principles of participatory practice in the following ways:

1. Use every opportunity to inquire about how the workplace runs and how it affects our lives. Investigate the ordinary. Practice asking questions and getting them answered. The questions may not necessarily derive from a particular workplace problem. In fact, many teachers note that workers resist bringing such problems to the classroom either because they do not feel safe in that group or,

sometimes, because they are already looking up and out to a future that does not include that workplace. Asking questions about one's environment, however, serves adults wherever they go. Some useful starting points, besides those that workers raise, include the following:

- Why does management think you need this class? What abilities do you have that management doesn't know about?
- Who has access to information and how do you get it (formal and informal routes)?
- What's a "good" job here? How do you define that?
- How do you get promoted here (the official and unofficial routes)?
- What is the history of this workplace? (Create a timeline of the organization, charting the size of the workforce, its ethnic make-up, organizational changes, etc.)
- Make a map the workplace (tracing the work process, noting the demographics of who works in which areas, marking health and safety dangers, etc.)

2. Seek to make and understand connections. These might be between individual and collective experience, specific concerns and the larger context, actions and consequences, or teachers and students as workers, who are in many ways struggling with the same issues of marginalized, insecure work. I share an example of this from some work I did with new practitioners. I was trying to generate discussion about the worker identity we share with our students. Adapting an activity from Simon, Dippo and Schenke, I asked each person to think of a job they'd had and to list what they would have needed to become more productive in that job. I then asked them to sort the list into the items that related to their own changes and skill development ("more training," "a better attitude," "reading my training materials," etc.) and items that described other kinds of changes ("more information from the company," "more feedback on my work," "end of capitalism," "a more

comfortable workspace," etc.). When we came back to share and discuss the lists, we found that individual changes accounted for only about 25% to 30% of those needed. We used our observations as a way to begin talking about our own roles in emphasizing education as the primary means to an improved work life, when our own experiences were telling us something else. How could we more consciously use those experiences to inform our teaching, make connections, and build relationships with students?

3. Use the participatory approach flexibly, always trying to carry forward its purpose rather than its method. Many practitioners get stuck equating participatory education with a particular set of steps that result in certain kinds of public action. Many teachers, myself included, have spent years either hurrying toward premature actions of one kind or another, or apologizing for lessons that merely ended in a new awareness of a workplace dynamic. To hurry the process can backfire, however, leaving workers to carry out a teacher-fueled agenda and, perhaps, take risks that have not been properly weighed. This is in no way to ignore the fact that acting in the world and examining what results is a terrific learning process. But, contrary to some interpretations of the approach, I believe that getting to an explicit public action is not as central as developing a depth of understanding that can support informed action whenever it becomes appropriate.

4. Prioritize worker goals to learn concrete skills. Work with them to recognize and articulate the skills they are learning during nontraditional lessons. Some practitioners end each class with a group recap of the ways they have practiced language and literacy, problem solving, and "team" skills.

PROCESS IN ACTION

We see some of the possibilities of teaching with a participatory approach. In each of the three examples, workers became engaged in redefining the meaning of a problematic situation and, in so doing, redefining themselves in relation to their work, their colleagues, and their employers.

The first lesson comes from an advanced ESOL class in a unionized manufacturing company, taught by Adam Bolonsky. He reports that "the lesson was designed in response to a class request to learn more about the jobs in the front office and, also, in response to a management request that students meet front office managers in the hopes of opening better channels of communication between line workers and management". To start off, the group invited the Marketing Director to their class to interview her about her job. During the interview, she described her work in jargon that confused some students and frustrated others. After she left, the group discussed their reactions to what they referred to as "inside language," some with that angry edge that comes from feeling stupid or inadequate. The more they talked about it (what it is, why it's used, and when they themselves use it), the more they saw it as a tool that could be used, purposefully, to include or exclude. They concluded that when they hear inside language they should ask themselves, "Is the person using it because it is the language he or she uses everyday? Or is the person using it because he or she wants to keep me on the outside?". Their perspective on the manager's language use shifted from a view of it as an oral mastery that reminded them of the education they lacked to a view of it as a social discourse that serves many purposes other than communication. This understanding opened up a much wider array of options in dealing with it. Bolonsky says, "Some students want others to learn to speak in plain English, yet are unsure of how to make that wish clear or even what plain English is; other students want to learn how to translate inside language but are unsure of how to do so; still others want to learn those discourses which separate them from the jobs, privileges, and goals they desire". Rather than thinking about language as something you have in varying amounts, the workers started talking about language as a process that mediates relationships, a tool the manager may have used to create distance. And understanding more clearly how language can be used to privilege some groups and diminish others, the workers saw choices in how to respond. In their acknowledgment of the value of their "plain English," we can see how they reclaimed their own language patterns as they prepared to approach more confidently the company's "inside language."

In the second example, some hospital workers have come to their ESOL class with a familiar Monday complaint. They say they have too much work to do because the weekend shift hasn't been pulling its weight. Their teacher, Amy Battisti, responded by writing up a catalyst dialogue about supermarket workers in a similar situation. After one reading, the workers began relating the scene to their own experience, creating additional characters, and dramatizing what they believed would happen next. As they discussed it further, they realized the problem was primarily in the way work was being organized, divided, and waylaid. The focus moved off of allegedly lazy workers and onto an organizational issue, which suggested vastly different responses and solutions.

Rather than going with the workers' initial assessment of the situation, the teacher prompted the group to look at the issue in a bigger context, discussing who had the authority to plan and divide work, and how the lines of communication worked. In the end, they determined that efforts to change the work system were beyond what they wanted to take on at that point and chose not to take any public action. They had, though, redefined the issue from one that divided them as workers to one that supported their solidarity. Their discussion enabled them to examine the environment that nurtured these conflicts and to see it as a place to look when other issues arose.

It illustrates the authority students begin to take over their lives when presented with the opportunity—

> *I use a lot of literature in my classroom as a way to open doors and comfortably discuss workplace issues, so I looked for literature that dealt with fences, walls, barriers. We studied Robert Frost's "Mending Wall" ... and read a scene from "Fences" by August Wilson. Everyone wrote a story about a barrier that prevented or enabled her/him from doing something that she/he wanted to do. Then we looked specifically at walls in the workplace. People imagined the walls they meet everyday visible and invisible. Then we talked about the walls that we wanted to build or wanted to take down, and why. Once we started taking walls down we were ready to deal with specific talk of the merger. A huge wall between two hospitals was coming down and none of the workers were happy about it, but there was nothing that anyone could do to stop it, so we decided to study it. We did a compare and contrast chart. We looked at the differences and the similarities of the two places and tried to anticipate problems that might occur when two very different places become one. We wrote out questions about downsizing and reorganizing to ask supervisors and union representatives. We shared valuable information with one another and corrected a lot of misinformation. We laughed a lot. The next day, a student brought in a card with a Chinese character drawn on it which, translated, meant "crisis as opportunity." Despite their fears, the workers began to explore the merger as something potentially positive. They decided to put together a simple list of strategies that could give people a measure of control and self-direction during a time of great change. Out of this came, after many discussions, "Our Merger Survival Handbook." It included:*
>
> 1. *Remember the saying "crisis as opportunity" and keep a positive attitude and an open mind.*
> 2. *Gather information by asking questions rather than listening to gossip and rumours.*
> 3. *Become valuable to the workplace:*
>   - *let people know you're willing to try new things,*
>   - *inventory your skills,*
>   - *identify what new skills might be needed in the workplace and learn them (especially computer skills) or let people know you're willing and able to learn them, and*
>   - *brush up your basic skills in reading, writing, speaking, and math.*
> 4. *Update your resume and practice cover letters.*

5. *Start networking call friends to find out what's out there and keep an eye open for job opportunities.*

The workers were proud of their product and distributed the handbooks at their annual achievement ceremony, as well as through the union newsletter.

During this unit, students grew beyond their positions as victims of change to become leaders in their workplaces. Their recommendations may appear to have accommodated management's needs, but I see them as practical suggestions that make it loud and clear that workers owe no loyalty to this organization. Their enlarged perspectives allowed them to create alternatives and plan for the future, even as they were anxious about the present. They didn't change the situation, but they changed their relationship to it, feeling less in its grasp and better equipped to take care of themselves and each other.

SUMMARY

A participatory model is welcome in few workplace settings. Practitioners are often only able to weave it in, intermittently, with more traditional approaches. But this is true outside of workplace education as well, even though the language of "empowerment" and "student directedness" is everywhere. Adult education is generally oriented to preparing people to uncritically participate in the current work, school, and political systems. Many argue this is what adults say they want. Participatory education will continue to ask deeper questions to find out if this is *all* they want.

The term Adult Education means providing education to the adult and aged people who, somehow, had failed to receive the elementary education during their childhood. The effort of providing adult education in India has been in existence for the past several years, as it is one of the most important things in building an educated nation. Unless the adults realize the importance of education they would never understand the need to educate their progeny. Education is one of the stepping stones for building a strong nation. Hence adult education is promoted on a large scale in the Indian sub continent.

Adult education in India is mainly provided at night schools. These are situated in almost all the Indian cities and villages. The provision for imparting education has been made at night because most of the people are engaged during the day. Apart from the night schools, the government had also set up some libraries so that the adults can study more to become educated, not just literate. Adult education is included among the most important responsibilities of the Government, as the eradication of illiteracy has been one of the major national concerns of the Government of India since independence. The government launched the programme of Social Education, under the Community Development Programme in 1952, as part of the first Five Year Plan. In the recent times, the government has launched the programme called National Literacy Mission (NLM) for spreading adult education in India.

A large number of initiatives have been taken so far for providing adult education in India. A machinery comprising male and female Social Education Organisers at grass-roots level and a Chief Social Education Organiser has been created, apart from the Social Education Organizers` Training Centres (SEOTCs). The government has also established model community centres, rural libraries, Janata Colleges, youth clubs, mahila mandals and folk schools, for spreading adult education. The Council for Rural Higher Education was established and a Standing Committee of the Central Advisory Board of Education (CABE) on Social Education was also constituted in 1956. The Government also started a National Fundamental Education Centre for providing high-level training facilities to the adults. However, apart from the Indian government, a large number of NGOs have also been working to spread adult education in India and they have indeed done a great job so far.

❑❑❑

Bibliography

Apps, Jerold W. (1981) *The Adult Learner on Campus*. Chicago: Follet Publishing Co. Though some of the material may be dated, this book contains many useful examples of exemplary practices.

Belenky, Mary Field, Blythe McVicker Clinchy, Nancy Rule Goldberger, Jill Mattuck Tarule. (1997). *Women's Ways of Knowing*. New York: Basic Books. (Originally published 1986). This book, written in 1986 and recently re-released by a division of Harper Collins, is a classic on knowledge construction as applied to women.

Braidotti, Rosi, Ewa Charkiewicz, Sabine Hausler, Saskia Wieringa. (1994). *Women, the Environment, and Sustainable Environment*. London: Zed Books. This book asks the reader to examine assumptions about the meaning of progress and development.

Carfagna, Rosemarie. (1995 Spring). A Developmental Core Curriculum for Adult Women Learners. *New Directions for Adult and Continuing Education*, No.65. In this article, 'Women's Ways of Knowing' provides the theoretical framework for a core curriculum designed to meet the learning needs of women.

Collins, A., J. G. Greeno, and L. B. Resnick, *Environments for Learning*

Costa, Arthur, *What Human Beings Do When They Behave Intelligently and How They Can Become More So*. Paper presented by Arthur Costa, California State University, Sacramento. The author lists characteristics and behaviors exhibited by intelligent people.

Cranton, Patricia. (1996). *Professional Development as Transformative Learning.* San Francisco: Jossey-Bass.

Cross, Patricia, (1981). *Adults as Learners,* San Francisco: Jossey-Bass. This book is a relative 'oldie' but nonetheless a goodie.

Cruikshank, Donald R., Deborah L. Bainer, Kim K. Metcalf. (1995). *The Act of Teaching.* New York: McGraw-Hill, Inc.

Dixon, Nancy M., *The Organizational Learning Cycle: How We Can Learn Collectively.*McGraw-Hill Book Co., London, 1994.

Draves, William A. (1984). *How to Teach Adults* Kansas: The Learning Resources Network.

Droegkamp, Jan and Kathleen Taylor (1995 Spring). Prior Learning Assessment, Critical Self-Reflection, and Reentry Women's Development. *New Directions for Adult and Continuing Education,* No.65.

Edwards, Richard and Robin Usher. (1996). University Adult Education in the Postmodern Moment: Trends and Challenges. *Adult Education Quarterly,* Vol.47, No.1.

Gajdusek, Linda and Helen Gillotte. (1995 Spring). Teaching to the Developmental Needs of Nonmainstream Learners. *New Directions For Adult and Continuing Education,* No. 65.

Galbraith, Michael. (1992 April). Nine Principles of Good Facilitation. *Adult Learning,* P10-.

Goulden, Nancy Rost and Charles J. G. Griffin. (1997 Fall). Comparison of University Faculty and Student Beliefs about the Meaning of Grades. *Journal of Research and Development in Education,* Vol. 31, No. 1.

Havighurst, Robert. (1953) *Human Development and Education* New York: David McKay Company.

Heath, Shirley Brice. (1982) *Questioning at Home and at School: A Comparative Study.* Illinois: Waveland Press, Inc.

Hooks, bell. (1989) *Talking Back, Thinking Feminist, Thinking Black.* Boston: South End Press. This reflective and thoughtful book tells the story of one woman's exploration of feminism and race.

Howard Gardner's theory of multiple intelligences has forced us to re-examine our assumptions about 'smart'.

Johnson-Bailey, Juanita and Ronald M. Cervero, *An Analysis of the Educational Narratives of Reentry Black Women.* Adult Education Quarterly: Vol.46, No.3, Spring 1996.

Knowles, Malcolm,*Andragogy in Action*, Malcolm Knowles is considered by many to be the father of adult education theory and practice.

Knowles, Malcolm. (1980). *The Modern Practice of Adult Education: From Pedagogy to Andragogy.* New Jersey: Cambridge/Prentice Hall Regents.

Kuh, George D., C. Robert Pace, and Nick Vesper,*The Development of Process Indicators to Extimate Student Gains Associated with Good Practices in Undergraduate Education.* Research in Higher Education: Vol. 38, No. 4, 1997.

LePage-Lees, Pamela,*Exploring Patterns of Achievement and Intellectual Development Among Academically Successful Women from Disadvantaged Backgrounds.* Journal of College Student Development: Vol. 38, No. 5, Sept/Oct. 1997.

Marienau, Catherine, *In Their Own Voices: Women Learning About Their Own Development.* New Directions For Adult and Continuing Education: No. 65, Spring 1995.

Merriam, Sharan B. and Rosemary S. Caffarella,*Learning in Adulthood.* Jossey-Bass, San Francisco, 1991.

Reinsmith, William A., *Two Great Professors: Formidable Intellects with Affection for Students.* College Teaching: Vol. 42, No. 4, Fall 1994.

Sheared, Vanessa, *Giving Voice: An Inclusive Model of Instruction-A Womanist Perspective.* New Directions for Adult and Continuing Education, No.61, Spring 1994.

Shoenecker, Timothy S., Kathryn D. Martell, and Joseph F. Michlitsch*Divesity, Performance, and Satisfaction in Student Group Projects: An Empirical Study.* Research in Higher Education: Vol. 38, No. 4, 1997.

Sitler, Helen Collins, *The Spaced Lecture,* College Teaching, Vol. 45, No. 3, Summer 1997. This article describes a method for incorporating active learning into lectures.

Spool, Jared M., Tara Scanlon, Will Schroeder, Carolyn Snyder, Terri DeAngelo. (1997). *Web Site Usability.* North Andover, MA: User Interface Engineering.

Taylor, Kathleen and Catherine Marienau, *Bridging Practice and Theory.* New Directions for Adult and Continuing Education, No. 65, Spring, 1995.

Taylor, Kathleen, *Sitting Beside Herself: Self-Assessment and Women's Adult Development.* New Directions for Adult and Continuing Education: No. 65, Spring 1995.

Tennant, Mark and Philip Pogson, *Learning and Change in the Adult Years: A Developmental Perspective (Chapters 1-3).* Jossey-Bass Publishers, San Francisco,

Tice, Elizabeth T., *Educating Adults: A Matter of Balance.*Adult Learning, Vol.9, No. 1, Fall 1997.

Tough, A. M., *The Adult's Learning Projects: A Fresh Approach to Theory and Practice in Adult Learning.*Ontario Institute for Studies in Education, Toronto, 1979.

Turoczy, Cheryl, *Question Well to Teach Well.* Adult Learning, Vol.8, #5 & 6, p.22.

Vella, Jane. (1994)*Learning to Listen, Learning to Teach: The Power of Dialogue in Educating Adults* San Francisco: Jossey-Bass, Inc.

Walden, Phyllis, *Journal Writing: A Tool for Women Developing as Knowers.* New Directions for Adult and Continuing Education: No. 65, Spring 1995.

Walker, Deborah and Linda Lambert, *The Constructivist Leader: Chapter 1 - Learning and Leading Theory.*

Wright, John C., Susan Millar, Steve Kosciuk, Debra Penberthy, *Does Active Learning Cause Credible Differences in Student Competence?* Focus on Calculus: Issue No. 13, Fall 1997.

Index

A

Accelerated Female Literacy Programme, 29
Acculturation of Indians, 197
Adult and Continuing, 104
Basic Education, 3
Education hrough Voluntary Agencies, 10
Education, 7
Education in the Community, 47
Advisory Council for Adult and Continuing Education (ACACE), 108
Advocating for the Interests of Women, 224
African-Americans, 181
Stereotypes, 185
Analysis of the NSSO Sample Survey Data on Literacy, 24
Andragogy, 1
Autonomy of Self-Reward, 170

B

Bootstrapping, 156
Britain, 49

C

CANDORA, 210
Capability and Enterprise, 137
Central Advisory Board of Education (CABE), 240
Chicano Civil Rights Movement, 192
Citizen Action, 165
Action and Roles, 165
Involvement, 165
Participation, 71
Common Socioeconomic Factors, 200
Community, 109
Action Agencies (CAAs), 68
Apathy, 62
Based Adult Education, 226
Development, 48
Development Corporations (CDCs), 68
Based Adult Education, 45
Based Organizations (CBOs), 67
Competence, 142

Competition, 123
Conceptual Analyses, 124
    Characteristics, 121
    Pasts and Futures, 127
Continuing Education (CE), 1, 27
    Centres (CECs), 31
Creating an Atmosphere of Participatory Democracy, 152
Culture and Value Defined, 181

D

Dilemmas, Pitfalls and Personal Traits, 162
Dimensions, 123

E

Education for Adults, 105
Educational Attainment, 201
    Linkages, 126
Employment Discrimination, 202
Empowerment for Self-Sufficiency and Self-Confidence, 223
English as a Second Language (ESL), 3
    for Speakers of Other Languages, 3
    Language Learners (ELL), 3
Enhancing Local Empowerment, 153
Equalizing Power, 221
Equivalency Programmes (EPs), 32
Establishing an Ongoing Vehicle for Community Development, 153
Examples of Adult Education Programs, 7
External Groups, 217

F

Farmers' Functional Literacy Project, 8
Female Literacy, 22
Field Agent, 161
Formal, Non-Formal and Informal, 113
Forms of Adult Education, 4
Functional Learning, 168
    Literacy for Adult Women (FLAW), 9
    Context Approach, 229
Fundamental Elements in Community based Organizations, 221
Future Directions, 203

G

General Education Development (GED) Test, 3
Goals for the XI Plan,, 41
Gram Shikshan Mohim, 8
Group Needs and Decision Making, 74

H

Higher Education, 99
Historical Background, 182
Historically Related Educational Issues, 187, 194, 199
Human Resource Development, 47

I

Ideals, 120
and Fashions, 94
Illiteracy Size, 20
Income Generating Programmes (Agps), 32
Increasing the Potential of Individuals, 152
India, 14, 50
Individual Interest Promotion Programmes (Iipps), 32
Institutional vs. Community based Development, 55
Intellectual Growth, 5
Interdisciplinary Nature, 53
Interests, 213

J

Jan Shikshan Sansthan, 35

K

Kerala Shastra Sahita Parishad (KSSP), 26
Knowledge and Skill, 132

L

Learning Organization, 85
Society, 90
Life Enrichment Education (LEE), 38
Lifelong Education, 81
Education and Awareness Programme (LEAP), 41
Learning, 229
Literacy Campaigns, 28
Rate 1951-2001, 15
Status in Nine most Populous Countries, 14
Status in Some Asian Countries, 13
Local Leadership, 69

M

Mexican-Americans, 188
Minority Group Overview, 179

N

National Adult Education Programme (NAEP), 9, 34
Literacy Mission (NLM), 12, 25
Sample Survey Organisation (NSSO), 25
Native Americans, 195
Negotiation, 219
Neighborhood Organizations, 66
Nigeria, 50
NLM - An Assessment,, 38
Nodal Continuing Education Centre (NCEC), 38
Non-Formal Education (NFE), 34

O

Organizational Levels, 125
Organizer's Roles, 160
Organizing Goals, 152
vs. Developing, 158
Other Asian Countries, 14

P

Participatory Approach, 231
Pedagogy, 1
Personal and Community Enrichment Program, 212
Growth and Development, 5
Perspective, 178
Plain English, 237

Policy, 119
Political and Practical
    Considerations, 171
    Battleground, 148
Politics of Local Control, 64
Polyvalent Adult Education
    Centres Workers, 8
Popular Education, 51
Post-Literacy Programme
    (PLP), 27
Poverty, 200
Power Relationships, 218
Principles and Procedures of
    Organizing, 154
    of Adult Education, 6
Process and Task
    Orientations, 52
    in Action, 235
Programmes under National
    Literacy Mission,, 28
Providing Opportunity for
    Learning and Problem
    Solving, 153
Purposes for Adult Education,
    5
Putting the Three Themes
    Together, 224

Q

Quality, 146
    of Life Improvement
    Programmes (Qlips), 32
Quest for Empowerment, 173

R

Review of the National Adult
    Education Programme, 10
Rural Functional Literacy
    Project (RFLP), 10

S

Seed of Creation, 154
Social Education, 8
    Education Organizers'
    Training Centres, 240
    Improvement, 5
    Learning, 57
    Transformation, 6
    Variables, 124
Space, 118
Staff at Candora, 215
State Adult Education
    Programme (SAEP), 10
    Groupings, 19
Status of Literacy among SCs
    and STs, 23
Stereotypes of Mexican-
    Americans, 193
Strengths, 11

T

Tensions, 121
    Traditions and
    Dichotomies, 115
The Basics, 3
    Focus on Learning, 168
    Organizer, 159
Theory, 120
Time, 117
Total Literacy Campaign
    (TLC), 26
Training and Development, 1

W

Weaknesses, 11
Women of Candora, 213

Z

Zilla Saksharata Samities
    (ZSS), 28